TWO KINDS OF VALUES

TWO KINDS OF VALUES

by L. M. LORING

Foreword by
Karl R. Popper

LONDON

ROUTLEDGE & KEGAN PAUL

First published in 1966
by Routledge & Kegan Paul Ltd
Broadway House, 68–74 Carter Lane
London, E.C.4

Printed in Great Britain
by Cox & Wyman, Ltd
London, Fakenham and Reading

CONTENTS

CONTENTS

FOREWORD

by Karl R. Popper

Miss Loring's interesting and challenging book is, most emphatically, *not a treatise on Ethics*; it is a treatise on non-ethical values. The point cannot be stressed too strongly, for it may easily be overlooked; first, because much in the book has important bearings on ethical theory and practice; secondly because the author, in order to bring out her distinction between non-ethical and ethical values, finds it necessary also to discuss the latter ones, in order to elucidate the former—the non-ethical values which are her main interest here.

It may be useful for a prospective reader to get this important point quite clear at the outset. For the author proposes *no* ethical thesis whatever. On the contrary, her first and central thesis is that there exist *non-ethical standards of value*—or, if you like, standards of non-ethical value—and that these non-ethical standards are in common use. A secondary thesis is that these non-ethical standards, which are of wide application, can provide us with a value system wide enough to make possible a rational and fruitful discussion, and an evaluation, of even those value systems usually called 'ethical' or 'moral'.

Now this brief formulation may sound, at first, a little tricky, or perhaps even confused; yet the idea is quite straightforward, and may be explained more fully as follows.

Everybody knows that there are good watches and bad watches, good motor-cars and bad motor-cars, good dentists and bad dentists, good agreements and bad agreements, where 'good' and 'bad' do not denote ethical values but values such as 'well made'. or in the case of the dentists perhaps, 'well trained for the purpose' or 'efficient'. Similarly we have good and bad meat, good and bad administrations and administrators, good and bad laws and judges. In most of these cases we speak of goodness and badness without attributing to these things or persons ethical values. What, then, are we saying? Miss Loring's answer is that we are in such cases attributing *some kind of beneficence* (or else some kind of *harmfulness*, or 'counter-beneficence') to these things or persons. She argues that these attributions of beneficence or harmfulness are based on a broad common fund of experience, and on universal assumptions about certain basic kinds of experiences which anyone wants to have or wants to avoid. Thus these attributions contain useful information; they are capable of being rationally discussed; and—in their appropriate contexts—they are up to a point empirically testable. For example, whether a proposed surgical operation is good or bad—beneficent or harmful—is, in principle, objectively decidable, and taken by everybody to be so. It may even be decidable whether it is the best kind of treatment available for a certain malady. Thus the universality which belongs to this type of non-ethical value statement may enable us to determine how to act 'for the best', as we say.

Now take my example of good and bad administrators or judges. It is very important to distinguish between a good—that is, a satisfactory—administrator (or judge) on the one hand, and, on the other hand, one who is morally or ethically good, that is, anxious to do his moral duty, though he may be unsatisfactory as an administrator (or judge); for example, because he is badly trained, or scatterbrained.

Here we have, clearly, two kinds of value which it is important to distinguish since they are in danger of being muddled up.

Take the famous story of Solomon judging the two women who were quarrelling about the child. Was Solomon a good judge? No doubt he was a marvellously clever and satisfactory lie-detector. But much more than this is demanded of a good judge; and something different still of a 'wise' judge and a good man.

So far everything is plain sailing: it is clear that there are non-ethical evaluations in common use; and it is also clear that they might sometimes be confounded with ethical evaluations. But one might think that the distinction is easy. The goodness of a good judge—a satisfactory judge—is a non-ethical value, and so may be his wisdom. Yet the goodness of a good man, one is inclined to say, will be moral or ethical goodness. In fact, something like this seems to be widely assumed by ethical writers.

Yet it is precisely here, I think, that Miss Loring has something new and important to say, and something which is perhaps not quite easy to grasp.

First of all, it is quite clear that a man may be a very good man without being morally good in the sense of the Ethics of the great philosopher Immanuel Kant. For a man may be *by inclination* benevolent, well-meaning, unselfish, tender-hearted; he may enjoy nothing more than to be kind to people, helpful, loving, ready to defend the weak, open and straight-forward. A man like this will, then, rarely, or never, do any-thing which Kant would classify as *immoral*; yet he will not be morally 'good' or 'virtuous' in the sense of Kantian Ethics —unless, indeed, he is a man who originally was possessed by 'bad' inclinations and who had to train himself to suppress these, and succeeded by his own efforts in replacing them by these 'good' inclinations. His act of self-education would be ethically or morally 'good' (in Kant's sense) if he acted against his inclinations and out of a sense of duty. But all those actions towards which he was moved by his 'good' inclinations (whether inborn or acquired) would be, according to Kant, ethically neutral—neither good nor bad. For only actions done for the sake of duty, rather than out of benevolent inclination, can be 'good' in Kant's sense.

This is of course a well-known stumbling-block of Kantian Ethics. It was first discovered by Kant's greatest disciple, the poet Friedrich Schiller, who wittily expressed his misgivings, as Miss Loring reminds us, in the form of two elegiac couplets which I may perhaps here translate:

Lovingly serve I my friends; yet I do so from fond inclination:
Thus no virtue is mine, and I feel greatly aggrieved.
What can be done about this? I might teach myself to detest them,
And, with disgust in my heart, serve them as duty commands.

As Miss Loring emphasizes, Kant made it quite clear that 'good will' in his terminology does not mean a *benevolent* will, but only a will that is inspired by the *sense of duty*. This Kantian use of 'good' is, in fact, the key-example of Kant's distinction between ethical and non-ethical evaluation. What Miss Loring has done is to re-discover this Kantian distinction, to elaborate it, to show its significance, and turn it to her own use—with a general outlook on human life which is very different from Kant's. One may perhaps formulate her attitude as follows: she fully accepts Kant's *demarcation* between 'ethical' (or 'moral') and non-ethical evaluations, but she declines to follow Kant when he assumes dogmatically that 'ethical' values are by their very nature superior, or more sublime, than non-ethical ones.

Thus it is the status of non-ethical values which is defended in this book; and non-ethical values are here given a certain priority over those ethical values whose supremacy is so often taken for granted.

It should be emphasized that it is *only* in order to bring out more sharply her basic distinction between ethical and non-ethical valuation that Miss Loring revives and adopts the Kantian conception of what is specifically ethical, and *not* because she has any sympathy with Kant's puristic or rigoristic views on conduct. Though she does not discuss her preferences, one feels that they would be for those non-ethical values like benevolence or beneficence which Kant so rigorously excluded.

The reader who is anxious to classify Miss Loring's views under one of the main traditional headings might be inclined to set her down as a member of the Utilitarian school. But this would be a grievous mistake. Admittedly, Miss Loring's practical preferences seem to have a great deal in common with those of the Utilitarians. *But she is very far from accepting anything like the Utilitarian ethical theory*. Utilitarianism agrees with Kantianism in declaring that it is the *duty* of everybody to *act benevolently*, that is, to act so as to render benefits to human beings (and perhaps even to animals). Now Miss Loring also values benevolence and beneficence very highly; and in the emphasis upon these values there is little difference between her views and those of the Utilitarians or of Kant.

But there is a great difference in the theory, and this difference is important because many people who value benevolence and beneficence are far from convinced that either Kant or the Utilitarians have produced sound theoretical arguments in favour of their ethical doctrines.

However this may be, seen from Miss Loring's point of view Utilitarianism proceeds, like Kantianism, first by adopting a non-ethical value, such as benevolence, and then by *making an ethical value out of it*—that is to say, a *duty*: it is our *duty*, according to Utilitarianism, to maximize benefits and minimize harm.

Yet benefit and harm are, in the first instance, *non-ethical* values and disvalues. As both Kant and the Utilitarians realized, animals and men by and large seek what is for their benefit and shun what is harmful, and they do it either quite spontaneously or as a matter of planned expediency. Kant was clear and definite in his insistence that acting from such motives was never moral and at best ethically neutral: nevertheless he said it was our duty to act for the *benefit* of others. Some Utilitarians tried to establish the view that what is expedient *is* moral, or one's *Duty*. Thus, seen from the point of view of the present book, both proceeded by taking the *non-ethical* values and disvalues of beneficence and harmfulness and building them in different ways into their ethical systems.

Now this *elevation* of certain *non-ethical values into ethical values* is a curious process which cannot be properly understood without first making clear the *distinction between the two kinds of values*. It is the main task of Miss Loring's book to make this distinction clear.

Only when this distinction has been made can we see that *ethical* goodness or badness, or rightness or wrongness, is in principle independent of the non-ethical values and disvalues of benefit and harm. Indeed, it is possible to take any non-ethical value *or disvalue* and elevate it into an ethical one, by declaring it to be our *duty* to act so as to support this value or disvalue.

Take harmfulness, for example: some people, such as Tolstoy (in *The Kreuzer Sonata*) have proposed an ethics which would make it 'good' in the ethical sense, and thus our 'duty', to work for the disappearance of mankind; not, as one might perhaps think, in order to put an end to *human suffering* (that would be a different problem) but in order to put an end to *human sinning*. This, they believe, can be done (because of original sin) only by eliminating the human race.

This example shows that there may be an *ethical* 'good' which obviously is 'bad'—that is, harmful—from the point of view of that *non-ethical* valuation which equates 'good' with 'beneficent to mankind'.

Miss Loring's sympathies, so far as *practical* questions of conduct are concerned, may be not far from the Utilitarian doctrines (or perhaps even from that Kant who said that we should work for other people's happiness and our own perfection—'perfection' meaning here that we improve ourselves so much that we act benevolently out of inclination); but they are clearly far removed from the teaching of such supermen as Nietzsche. Her *theoretical* approach, as emphasized by herself, owes everything to Kant's demarcation of Ethics, but is in other respects very different from Kant (and even more from the Utilitarians); but it has, I think, some similarities with Nietzsche: what she calls 'moralism' has some similarities with what Nietzsche attacked, and what he sometimes called by a similar name; and Nietzsche's attempt to find a system of values 'beyond Good and Evil' (that is, the *ethical* Good and Evil), has similarities with Miss Loring's attempt to use her non-ethical system of valuation for evaluating ethics. But while Nietzsche dreamed of an *élite* which practices new and *nobler* (because non-hypocritical) standards of conduct, the aim of Miss Loring's present book is not to uphold any ideal or principle of conduct, but purely *to disentangle non-ethical from ethical evaluation*. She hopes that in this way when we discuss things, events, actions, people, policies, institutions, thought-conventions, or anything else, in terms of goodness and badness, we shall know better what we are talking about, and what kind of evidence is, or is not, relevant to our arguments.

I

ETHICAL AND NON-ETHICAL EVALUATION

*We need not wait for the Moralist's verdict before
calling one kind of action good and another bad.*

LAN FREED

SUMMARY: There are in common use two distinct systems
of evaluation, *both applicable to conduct*. These I describe as
(a) *ethical* and (b) *non-ethical* (somewhat arbitrarily but, I
argue, justifiably). By my classification *ethical* evaluation
is based on the idea of *Duty*, in the Kantian sense, and
on the closely associated ideas of *absolute* 'rightness' and
'wrongness' and the categorical 'Ought'. The system of
non-ethical evaluation I am concerned with here is based
on ideas of *benefit* and *harm* (notions whose origin will be
examined in Chapter 2). It is possible so to distinguish
between these two methods of evaluating conduct that
ethical 'goodness' and 'badness'—or moral 'rightness' and
'wrongness'—are recognized as essentially independent
of ideas of what is *beneficent* or *harmful*; whilst *non-ethical*
goodness and badness—or beneficence and harmfulness—
are essentially independent of ideas of what is, *ethically-
speaking*, 'good' or 'bad'—i.e. morally 'right' or 'wrong'.
Non-ethical evaluation in terms of beneficence and
harmfulness is universally applicable not only to conduct,
but to *any things or events as they are seen to affect human interests*.

I

The distinguishing mark of a moral action is not that it does
good, or even that it is intended to do good, but that the agent
believes it is his moral Duty to do it, regardless of its results.
This was Kant's view, and although it may well seem repug-
nant it is very difficult to reject it on any logical grounds, as

I hope to show. Its consequences in ethical theory are certainly
important, for if morality essentially consists in doing what a
sense of Duty dictates, then a bad (maleficent) action may in
principle be just as much a moral action as a good (beneficent)
one, and even the most monstrous deeds are morally Right if
inspired by a sense of Duty. (Kant made titanic efforts to
outlaw this unwelcome conclusion from his own ethical
premise, but in vain.)

The above considerations are often used as a reason for
rejecting Kant's condition for what he called 'moral value' by
those who, following the Utilitarians, cling to the idea that it
must be 'morally right' to act beneficently, or that benevolent
motives *must* be 'morally right' motives. But this is ultimately a
matter of classification; and mistaken classification, I believe.
To me the philosophical importance of Kant's doctrine lies
precisely in the fact that it marks out for us clearly and uncom-
promisingly the two alternative ways in which actions can be—
and habitually are—evaluated; such that one and the same
action may be 'good' or 'right' in the purely *ethical* sense, as
being *dictated by Duty*, yet at the same time 'bad' in the non-
ethical sense as being *harmful or conducive to suffering*. And
similarly, that one and the same action may be ethically-
speaking 'bad' or 'wrong' as being *contrary to what Duty required*,
but 'good' as *beneficent*.

In my view there is a lot to be said for recognizing this
distinction, and for considering its powers of clarification,
which are greater than may appear at first sight. For if, as I
shall argue, there really is an established mode of evaluation
which is strictly non-ethical, in that it *owes nothing* to the Duty-
criterion or the distinctively ethical notion of unconditional
moral 'rightness', but which is derived instead from broadly-
based ideas of *beneficence* and *harmfulness*, then it seems as if
we must have here a critical apparatus which could be used
to evaluate not only motives and actions but also modes of
thought, doctrines, and even conduct-principles, purely as they
affect, or tend to affect, the 'weal or woe' of sentient beings.
(It seems preferable to call this mode of evaluation 'non-
ethical', not 'non-moral', simply because 'moral' is apt to be
used in so many senses that have nothing at all to do with
Ethics proper. Admittedly 'ethical' is also used in various loose

ways, but at least there are respectable precedents for adhering to the stricter meaning, such that '*non*-ethical' means '*not* derived from the concepts of Duty, the categorical "ought", or unconditional moral "rightness".')

The rest of this chapter is the first stage in my argument for the following proposition: That the proposition, '*The practice of evaluating motives and conduct according to the criterion of Duty or "moral rightness" does more harm than good*' and its contrary, '*The practice of evaluating motives and conduct according to the criterion of Duty or "moral rightness" does more good than harm*' are *reasonable* and *arguable* propositions. Later I shall analyse and discuss the effects of what I call *Moralism*—the name I give to the mode of thought and discourse which results from *blurring-over the distinction between ethical and non-ethical values*.

2

To criticize one set of ethical ideas by the value standards belonging to another is considered to be quite an intellectually respectable activity: and so it is. But anyone who set out to evaluate in a comprehensive way the *whole body* of ethical thinking—to discuss whether it is on balance a good or a bad way to approach our problems of conduct—would most likely find himself classed with the absent-minded sage who puts on his spectacles in order to search for them.

'Any *evaluative* criticism of Ethics as a whole, any criticism that is not a mere matter of logical analysis,' he would be told, 'must obviously be based on a system of values that you yourself accept. So your criterion for criticism would necessarily be contained within the very thing you were trying to criticize!'

Though it is not by any means the chief purpose of this book to undertake the critical enterprise in question, I do dispute the above objection to it. It would be sound enough if all values were, in fact, ethical values, but this I deny; and I am sure that any morally-minded layman would also deny it, even in the teeth of what moral philosophers may ingeniously argue. For it would be obvious to him that many of the assertions of goodness, badness, and so forth that he makes about things and events in the ordinary course of conversation are not even remotely connected with his ideas of what is morally right or wrong, or of what *ought*, morally-speaking, to be; or of Duty. How far it may be appropriate, or even possible, to apply the same kind of value standards that we use when talking of such commonplace things as food and clothes and the weather, when we are considering matters of great moment, such as human inter-relations and the principles and policies that help to determine them, is another question—I shall return to it later. Just now I only want to make the point that it is at least reasonable to regard certain values as lying outside the field of Ethics. I also claim that it is eminently sensible and convenient; for to argue, as some philosophers have done, that even such value judgements as we pass on inanimate objects or events beyond our control are somehow basically 'ethical', is surely to deprive the very idea of Ethics of all distinctiveness. So if only for this reason, I think it is best to accept the severe limits which some moral philosophers set to the class of value judgements which, they claim, belong properly to Ethics.

To accept these limits, however, is not to accept the point of view or the assumptions of those who set them. It so happens that the upholders of ethical 'rigour' have usually been inspired not only by considerations of logic, but also by the belief that the world would be a better place if we all tried to act in accordance with their strict principles. I am very far from sharing that belief.

3

All moral philosophers of the school of Kant, as well as most upholders of particular moral principles, consider that the business of Ethics is with *ethical* values, in the strict and distinctive sense of 'ethical'; that is with the values attached to ideas of Duty, moral 'rightness' and 'right' principles, and kindred matters; and they deny emphatically that those other values which have to do with tastes and preferences, likes and dislikes, have any place at all in its domain—except in the sense that they provide us with alternatives to 'moral choices'. Ethical theory *takes account* of them, but they have no ethical status themselves.

This view is much less widespread than it used to be; and

nowadays the frontiers of the realm of Ethics are so ill-defined that there is a large, if uncertain, area of agreement among moral philosophers of very different persuasions. Probably the sharpest difference over values is still that between the heirs of Kant and Bentham respectively, at least as regards actions. The Kantian, or anyhow the consistent Kantian, denies that the ethical or moral value of an action—its *Goodness*—has anything at all to do with whether it is a *beneficent* action. The Benthamite says that on the contrary it has everything to do with this, and that if an action doesn't *do* good it is not good in any sense at all. These two schools of thought agree at least in making *conduct* the main concern of Ethics, but in between them, though with a perceptible slant towards Bentham's side, there has sprung up under the stimulus of G. E. Moore's *Principia Ethica* a school of value-dialectics in which the very subject of actions and motives tends to disappear under a thicket of arguments about the meanings and the uses of value terms, though it is still claimed that the subject of all this verbal analysis is 'Ethics'. This approach has produced confusion about both the nature of evaluation and the nature of Ethics, as I shall later try to show.

4

The main advantage of adopting a strict and narrow view of what sort of value judgements are, and are not, to be regarded as proper to Ethics is that this makes it possible for the moral philosopher to treat Ethics as a sharply defined study or discipline by centring it upon a concept that everyone accepts as being *exclusive* to Ethics; namely DUTY. Duty, not this duty or that, but Duty plain; Duty as apostrophized by Wordsworth in his *Ode to Duty*; Duty in the sense of Kant when he insisted that to be moral an act must be done *from* Duty—Duty in this way intended is almost the only term whose meaning is purely, unequivocally, *ethical*. ('Sin' perhaps also qualifies, but it has more restricted, theological, connotations.) Terms such as right, wrong, good, and bad, which figure so prominently in ethical discourse all have senses which, so at least it can be strongly claimed, are not ethical at all. Kant pointed out that even the word 'ought' has a non-ethical as well as an ethical meaning. But Duty is the sovereign ethical concept, whose peculiar and distinctive status is beyond dispute.

5

Because of its uniqueness, the concept of Duty can provide us with a sort of touchstone to decide the meaning of value terms as we use them, enabling us to tell when they do, and do not, carry an ethical or 'moral' meaning, in the strict Kantian sense. The test is simply to find whether or not the term in question stands for a concept related to the central ethical concept of Duty. So on this principle, if you say that a certain action was wrong or bad you are passing an *ethical* judgement *only* if you are ready to translate your words into the statement that it was the agent's Duty to do something else instead, or that his doing the action was contrary to his Duty. Otherwise the meaning could merely have been that the action was mistaken, or unsuitable to the situation, or that it harmed somebody; not that it was 'morally wrong'.

In the same way, if you say that some action was good or right you are using good—or right—in the strict *ethical* sense *only* if you mean to say that the person who did it was thereby doing his Duty. Further, if you say that something ought to be done, meaning that it is somebody's Duty to do it you are speaking in properly *ethical* terms; and even if you say only that something ought to *be*, your meaning is properly *ethical* if you mean that it is somebody's Duty, or that it is the Duty of man, to try to bring it about, but not otherwise.

(What notions the concept of Duty itself involves are discussed in Chapter 4.)

6

Philosophers who are not interested in discriminating between ethical and non-ethical value judgements about actions usually allow Duty only a secondary role in their hierarchy of ethical concepts. In Moore's *Principia Ethica* for instance, it is laid down that 'Our "duty" . . . can only be defined as that action which will cause more good to exist in the Universe than any possible alternative'. Thus according to Moore the idea of 'duty' is dependent on the idea of 'good'. In Kant's system, by contrast, it is the other way round: the 'goodness' of Kant's 'good will' consists in its being moved to action by the recognition of Duty alone.

Because of his insistence that 'good', not Duty, is the supreme ethical concept Moore could not find any other standard for ethical goodness than existing tastes and preferences: his own, and by inference other people's. He asserted, in fact, that certain experiences, which he specified, are by far the best, the most 'worth having purely for their own sakes'[1], and that really everybody must on reflection agree about this. But even supposing Moore had been right, a Christian or a Kantian moral philosopher would say, with some logical justification, surely, that what Moore regarded as ethical value in an object is not properly speaking ethically determined at all, but is simply a matter of taste or liking; and that even if everybody in the world happened to favour certain things, or could learn to favour them, this would have nothing whatsoever to do with whether they were *ethically* good, or with the extent to which, if so, they were so. For Ethics is concerned not with what is, or what might be, but with what OUGHT, morally, to be. Nobody interested in moral philosophy can afford to brush aside this view of the matter, which has been accepted and respected over a long and fertile period in the history of ethical theory. But it is very difficult to see how the view that *all* value judgements are *ethical* judgements could be possibly be reconciled with it—which is another reason why it seems advisable, even for those of us who are not Ethicists, to recognize a clear dividing-line between ethical and non-ethical evaluation.

7

Didactic Ethicists who follow Kant in making Duty the supreme ethical concept from which all pure ethical values spring, enjoy a special advantage in that they recognize with Kant that there are non-ethical as well as ethical criteria of value—though perhaps they might, on reflection, feel some doubt whether to exploit it. The advantage is that by accepting this situation they enable themselves to put forward *non*-ethical arguments in

[1] *Principia Ethica* (C.U.P.) p. 188.

favour of Duty. If they are not content simply to go on repeating in a reverent tone that Duty just *is* supreme, they will have to find some way of claiming in value terms that it is so. In other words, they will have to be able to argue that Duty is in some way or other supremely *good*, or *beneficent*. Now since they hold that all proper *ethical* value judgements depend ultimately on the idea of Duty they obviously can't apply an *ethical* value criterion to Duty itself. But they can still make use of whatever *non*-ethical value criterion they recognize, and so, for instance, contend that Duty is supremely good because, say, it is only through our sense of it that we ever control our natural ferocity and behave in a humane and civilized way. Even the most austere Ethicists are apt to use this sort of appeal as a matter of course, but it is interesting, and at first sight surprising, that Kant, the great apostle of pure Duty, should have had recourse to it. Kant wrote of the majesty and sublimity of Duty—and that was all very well. But he also often used instances to show that acting from Duty was a thoroughly sound policy, a good thing all round; and this even though the last thing he ever intended was to concede that non-ethical judgement had, as it were, any right to a say in the matter. (Passages from Kant have been cited to prove that he merely meant to say that by a kind of lucky accident truly moral conduct happened to be socially desirable conduct as well—but, as will presently be seen, this was by no means the whole story.) Such lapses on the part of Kant show very forcibly that the Ethicist, the champion of Duty, is obliged to introduce what he himself regards as non-ethical evaluative judgements if ever he wants to *recommend*, and not merely to *exalt*, his supreme ethical principle. It is this complicated situation, and the wish to get round it, which is largely responsible for that embranglement of value concepts which I shall later discuss under the title of Moralism.

8

Moralism, in brief, is the name I give to that mode of thought and that type of ethical discourse which confuses strictly ethical or moral value-concepts—viz. those derived from the idea of Duty—with those other value concepts which relate to our ideas of the beneficent and the harmful, the expedient and the inexpedient, which I treat as basically *non*-ethical. (A language difficulty crops up here, because although I have applied the term 'ethical' to *judgements* in the strict—i.e. Kantian—sense which excludes those judgements which are independent of the idea of Duty, usage makes it necessary to designate as 'Ethics' the *whole* subject-matter with which the moral philosopher deals, including various forms of what I call Moralism. Because of this difficulty I shall write 'strict Ethics' or 'strictly ethical' wherever this may be necessary so as to avoid ambiguity. For similar reasons I write 'Ethicist' where 'Moralist' would normally be used, and only use 'Moralist' to distinguish those, e.g. the Utilitarians, whose doctrines come under my head of Moralism.)

9

Kant has often been accused of inconsistency for introducing expediency-values into his system of 'pure' Ethics; and I think the accusations are justified. But the particular point I want to stress here is that in bringing a non-ethical value criterion to the support of Duty—even though unintentionally—Kant was undermining that very supremacy he claimed for it. And this is where I come back to my original subject—the critical evaluation of ethical ideas. For whatever is not 'beyond all praise' is not beyond all dispraise either; and what is subject to evaluation at all is in principle open to adverse no less than to favourable verdicts. The same sort of consideration applies wherever non-ethical value judgements are brought to the assistance of ethical ones.

As it happens, this threat to the unique immunity from criticism which ethical evaluation claims to enjoy has seldom been noticed by moral philosophers of any school, because their usual attitude towards whatever *non*-ethical value criteria they notice is that they are negligible or contemptible or both. Kant treated certain values as non-ethical on purely philosophic grounds, but because he was a strict Ethicist by temperament, as well as a philosopher, he freely expressed his poor view of them. His general attitude appears to have been that any values which are unconnected with the lofty conception of

Duty are ignoble, and that any which are connected with passions and appetites are quite deplorable.

The wide and various class of those moral philosophers who, though they reject Kant's strict demarcation of the ethical field, do not go all the way with Bentham and Spencer in claiming the *whole* of evaluation for Ethics, usually regard such non-ethical value criteria as they recognize as being not so much ignoble or deplorable as simply uninteresting. Certainly, they will concede, we often pass non-ethical value judgements —as when we speak of good and bad eggs. But this sort of judgement is not at all important because it has no bearing, or very little bearing, on conduct. So for one reason and another the tendency is to neglect or disparage non-ethical evaluation, and the idea that it might be used for any kind of critical assessment of purely ethical values, or even of the whole system of ethical evaluation, seems hardly to occur to anyone.

10

In general it seems to be taken as almost axiomatic that no matter how wide or how narrow is the claim that any particular ethical system may have staked out in the whole field of evaluation there is no possible *non*-ethical vantage-point from which that system could ever be criticized *in value terms*. Yet this is odd in a way, seeing that the moral philosopher, when he looks at various and partly conflicting ethical systems—say the Buddhist, the Communist, and the Christian—is often ready to claim that one of them is better than the others; and he would certainly deny that by calling it better he merely means that he, personally, happens to prefer it. So it would seem that unless he is deceiving himself, he must be judging by an independent criterion. The truth of the matter is, I believe, that an independent criterion is very often being used unawares, and that this goes for many sorts of judgement that are supposedly ethical.

Now accepting the Kantian view that ethical and non-ethical evaluation are *entirely different* in kind, I am going to argue that non-ethical evaluation, far from being trivial or purely subjective, plays a vitally important part in our communications. Here and now I claim that its scope is wider than that of ethical evaluation, because non-ethical value statements, besides being applicable to a number of things to which ethical evaluations are irrelevant, can encompass Duty and the moral Ought; and ethical value statements cannot.

So now let us turn to the class of non-ethical value statements, and consider what they mean, and what they are for.

2

THE WIDE SCOPE OF
NON-ETHICAL EVALUATION

The goodness of good objects consists in the possibility of their leading to some realization of directly experienced goodness.

C. I. LEWIS

SUMMARY: The significance of value statements is not to be found by treating good as an entity in itself, or 'goodness' as an intrinsic property of objects; nor yet by equating all value statements with *ethical judgements*, or interpreting them as expressions of *personal feelings* or *emotional attitudes*. I argue that the most common type of value statement used as *communication* derives its meaning from a universal assumption here called the *basic-values assumption*. This is the assumption that certain *basic types of experience* (for which we have names) are universally *liked* or *sought*, and that certain other basic types of experience (also named) are universally *disliked* or *shunned*. In basic evaluation what is judged to conduce to the former type of experience is said to be *good*—i.e., beneficient—what is judged to conduce to the latter type is said to be *bad*—i.e. either harmful or, in my terminology, 'counter-beneficent'. On this interpretation that class of value statements which I call *basic* can be recognized as *impersonal*, and free of ethical connotations. *Basic evaluation can be used for the criticism of ethical evaluation.*

I

Hardly a day passes without one's hearing, or reading, that something is good or is bad, or is better or worse than something else; that this or that action did good or harm, or that it would be a good, or a bad, thing if this or that were to happen. It is this sort of statement that I want to examine in the present chapter, and discuss the role it plays in our communications: a consistent and important role, I shall argue.

There are many different ways of approaching the subject of value statements, and, to my mind, one of the least fruitful is to set out to discover some *essence* of value or worth which, when identified, will, it is hoped, reveal their true meaning. Such attempts, in the tradition of Plato and Aristotle, mostly concentrate on investigating the source of the idea of good, or 'the good', and it is usual to start by examining how the word 'good' is used in our normal conversation, with the idea that this will reveal what good or goodness ultimately *is*. But the trouble about this method is that if good is an essence or an intrinsic quality, and so independent of human judgement, human value statements, made in human terms, can never disclose its nature; and the most exhaustive study of all possible uses of the word 'good' won't necessarily take us any nearer to knowledge of it. Plato himself never made this mistake, and so it was much easier for him to be consistent, for he began and ended his analysis in the realm of metaphysics.

According to Plato goodness is always *relative*. He held that goodness is approximation to Perfection. Thus to say that something is good would, on this view, be to say that it resembles some ideal prototype. If a Platonist says that a particular man, for example, or harvest, or chair, is good he is saying that it is to some extent like the perfect man, or harvest, or chair. In these terms, as it happens, value statements could sometimes have a limited sort of testability. For if someone says that a particular chair, say, is a good one, a disciple of Plato could falsify this by pointing out that it is so far from perfect that it has a large broken hole through the seat. But naturally, Plato cannot tell us how to decide between the relative goodnesses of two *sound* chairs, nor how to decide whether either is entitled to be called good, for this could only be a matter of intuition. Therefore to suppose that this very limited and entirely arbitrary criterion has a bearing on our everyday value statements seems most unrealistic; especially when we consider that most of us learn to understand and use statements of goodness long before we have been introduced to the idea of perfection at all.

Another school of thought which tries to bring common usage to the support of a metaphysical true-essence theory derives from Aristotle, who held that goodness in anything was essentially the property of fulfilling its purpose. So this school teaches that when we say a thing is good we mean that it is in some way fitting, or suited to perform its proper function. In one respect this view comes closer to the facts of usage than does the other; for it seems to be true that when we assert goodness of a thing made by man for his own use we do as a rule imply that it serves his purpose well.

But the fact remains that we are in the habit of ascribing goodness not only to shoes, ships, sealing-wax, cabbages, and kings, but also to events—even quite accidental, unpurposed, events sometimes. 'It was a good thing,' we say, 'that the Foreign Secretary was in bed with 'flu', or, '—that the Foreign Secretary was well again'. Also, although we may call a *person* good, as performing his function satisfactorily, we may also say it with a more general meaning which leaves his function out of account. So I think that the 'instrumental' theory of value statements is *inadequate.* However, if only those who believe in versions of the Platonic or Aristotelian theories of evaluation would not try to argue from common usage, but would be content to use value terms in their own way among themselves there would be no reason to quarrel with them. It is only when a member of either school insists that all, or at any rate most, *ordinary* value statements mean what *his* mean, that we find it necessary to contradict him.

2

Apart from the metaphysicians and their disciples, those who theorize about the meaning and the uses of the value words 'good' and 'bad' can mostly be seen, according to their general attitude towards their subject, as belonging to one or the other of two schools which might be called respectively the Reverent, and the Aloof. Those of the Reverent school treat value language as of supreme importance because it is the language in which ethical judgements are pronounced. What characterizes almost all versions of this type of approach is the dogged attempt to house in one many-mansioned edifice just about everything in thought and language that relates to choices and preferences, motives, aims, and decisions of any and every kind, along with the stern, if shadowy, shapes of Duty, Ought, Right and Wrong, and Moral Obligation.

The implications and consequences of this way of treating value language I will leave for discussion in later chapters.

The Aloof, though they may or may not choose to classify value language as 'ethical' language, are not inclined to accord it any special place of honour among types of communication, though they differ considerably among themselves about the extent of its importance. One group declares that we call things good and bad in just the same spirit that a dog wags his tail or growls. Others hold, more generously, that this is only part of the story; for though it is true that we often use value words simply to give vent to our immediate feelings of liking and aversion we *also* use them for expressing more permanent emotions—or rather emotional attitudes—those, namely, which reflect the customs and taboos of our society. In this way value language can express the complacence of the conventional person when things go according to the rules, and his shocked feelings when the rules are flouted.

Yet another group within the Aloof school allows our assertions of goodness and badness an even richer significance than the above. This claims that besides giving us verbal equivalents for the smile and the scowl and also concise alternatives to the statements 'This I approve as being in conformity with the conventions of my society' and 'This I disapprove because it outrages the conventions of my society', statements of goodness and badness also carry a tacit demand that the hearer shall share the speaker's feelings, or sentiments, as the case may be. On this view the formula 'This is good' has the effect of saying 'I like'—or, 'I approve of—this, and I require you to like'—or 'to approve of—it too'. So by an ingenious verbal device we are able to use what sounds like, but is not really, a statement about the object referred to, to express at one and the same time an emotional reaction and a demand.

A fourth group, unlike the one just mentioned, are not merely aloof but positively contemptuous in their attitude to

value language. As well as saying that 'good' and 'bad' are
on a par with the noises and grimaces by which we may
express our feelings or our wish to command or persuade, they
explicitly refuse them the status of predicates, and deny that
the sentences in which they occur are ever proper statements
at all. This group was formerly composed of Logical Positivists,
but though their views have become modified in various ways,
their brand of value-word disparagement lives on. Theirs was
the severest attack of all, though some of the leading assailants
afterwards relented, and themselves applied salves to the
wounds.

3

All the various branches of the Aloof school agree in regarding
value language as essentially 'subjective'; and in my own
view that is their chief defect, since I do not think any version
of the subjectivist interpretation covers the facts of usage satisfactorily. Perhaps the most obvious objection is that if you
are going to deny any kind of objectivity to statements of
goodness and badness you have to ignore our familiar habit
of using them to give practical information about the things
they refer to, which happens whenever we use them as answers
to questions. (If asked, 'Is it a good one?' we say 'Yes', or 'Not
very', and so on.) But there is another fact which tells even
more strongly against subjectivism, though at first sight it
might actually seem to support it.

This is the fact that we often use value terms in expressions
of opinion, which do not even pretend to be factual statements.
We say we think it was very likely a good thing after all that
this or that happened, or that we are inclined to believe that
A's action probably did more harm than good; and we often
say such things in answer to a request for our opinion. Now
these diffident pronouncements are not spontaneous 'emotional
reactions', nor do they at all necessarily express fixed attitudes
of approval and disapproval. We make them as statements of
what we think may actually *be the case*, though without pre-
tending to certain knowledge. They occur in discussions,
against a background of shared assumptions, and they have
the same logical form as expressions of opinion and guesses

about events in the physical world. These are two points about the way we use value terms which, I think, make it reasonable to consider whether some value statements are not, after all, what they pretend to be—a kind of statement about objects, material or non-material, even though they are not directly about physical properties or physical effects.

As regards the view that value statements are 'meaningless': I shall not try either to support or to oppose this particular accusation, because the distinction which Logical Positivists used to draw between meaningful and meaningless utterances is irrelevant to my approach. According to the everyday view of meaning—which I hereby embrace—no word or sentence is necessarily meaningless as it stands. The expression 'kilowatt-hours' for example, though likely to be meaningless to anyone who has not had it explained to him, has a precise enough meaning for some people. And in the same way, 'fiddle-de-dee' might be pregnant with meaning among a group of children. Meaning in *communication*, which is the only sort I am concerned with here, depends upon what might be called the understanding-situation between speaker and hearer or reader and writer; and this situation may be broad enough to embrace the whole class of normal adult members of a group speaking the same mother tongue, or so narrow as to embrace only a couple of conspirators.

4

Setting aside now all those theories about value words which relate them to the *essential nature* of goodness and badness, or which treat them as components of ethical judgements, or which treat them as expressions of emotion, I want to draw attention to a wide and familiar range of value statements which I think may properly be regarded as *objective*: objective, that is, in the sense that they are not expressions of personal emotion or attitude, and that they genuinely make assertions about objects. But first it seems necessary to emphasize that I am not going to try to *define* the terms 'good' and 'bad', nor argue that statements containing them are always, or nearly always, of the kind I am concerned to discuss in this place. All I want to do is isolate for examination what I take to be

one recognizable form of value statement that we use and understand in our open communications.

By 'open' communications I mean those statements, questions, and expressions of opinion whose significance does not
depend on any special personal understanding between the
individual speaker and hearer, or reader and writer, but is
roughly the same for anyone who knows the language in which
they are uttered. The statements we make, or the questions
we address, to strangers are normally of this kind, and so are
writings for public consumption. By contrast, some of our
communications to members of our family or to friends or,
say, to members of our particular religious sect, are not.

Now, whenever we discuss anything—no matter what—we
imply by the very act of directing words at each other pur-
posively that we believe in certain basic resemblances in our
experience, and in our thinking about it, which these words
reflect. (Therefore it is quite unnecessary to agree beforehand
that we will not challenge certain fundamental assumptions,
such as that people think and feel. At the same time, however,
there is no harm in sometimes mentioning that we do make
these assumptions, because we may forget that we make them
—as is shown by such recurring fusses as, 'But what do we *mean*
by "meaning"?' or, 'But what reason have we for thinking
that anyone thinks?') The assumption that we can understand
each other is implicit in all our communications.

Closely related to our assumptions about each other's minds
is the taking for granted that we inhabit a world of things
which affect the senses of all of us in basically similar ways,
so that the names we give to them, and the descriptive terms
we apply to them stand for the same, or very similar, physical
experiences in the mind or imagination of anyone and everyone who is familiar with the language in which these terms
occur. Of course there is no telling whether our faith in this
community of experience is really justified. The simple fact is
that all normal people have it, and that it is the basis of all
our communications about what exists and what occurs in
the material world. (Victims of the mental disease called
schizophrenia suffer from a partial loss of this faith. People
who think, or pretend, that they lack it call themselves
solipsists.)

If we accept the view that this, literally, *common*-sense assumption underlies all our significant statements about the material world, *a fortiori* it must underlie all our significant *value* statements about that world. Unless I believe that the word 'apple' represents in your mind the same sort of experience —visual, tactile, and so on—that it does in my own I should not think there was any sense in telling you that a particular apple, or variety of apple, was a good one.

But what *is* the sense of my statement that the apple is good? Am I saying that it resembles the Perfect Apple? Or am I merely saying that I want to eat it? Or that as well as wanting to eat it I also want you to eat it? (There is an obvious practical difficulty here.) Or again, am I saying that apples like this one *ought* to be eaten? There seems no end to the theories that philosophers will think up in order to find the true inward significance of such a seemingly straightforward and commonplace assertion as that some object understood to have a particular use or function is a good one. Later I shall discuss some of these theories and give my reasons for rejecting them. Here I propose to put forward without more ado my own theory, which I believe to be free of various objections which apply to the others.

5

I suggest, then, that what distinguishes, and gives significance to, the most familiar form of open value statement is *another* universal assumption in addition to, or rather, superimposed upon, the common-sense one. This secondary assumption is that there are certain universal basic *tastes in experience*. This, for want of a better term, I call *the basic-values assumption*.

Before I come to my argument for the existence of the basic-values assumption I must first draw attention to a department of language which lies, as it were, *between* common-sense language and value-language, and forms a kind of bridge between them. I am referring to what can be broadly called *psychological* language—the language we use to denote mental and emotional states and experiences such as wishing, remembering, expecting, disliking, hoping, and so on.

As with the language of common sense, we take such terms

to apply to experience *universally*; thus whether I say that I am frightened, or that Mrs Smith is frightened, or that the Chinese are frightened I am understood to be saying essentially the same thing about the subject in every case. That this is a necessary feature of communication is perfectly obvious; but I have to stress it, because this universalizing and depersonalizing of psychological statements, showing that we assume the existence of *common types of mental experience, no less than of common types of sense-experience* is, I shall maintain, the foundation of whatever objectivity and universality may belong to value statements.

6

We have, then, this rooted belief in a great variety of mental and emotive experiences to which normal human beings are susceptible; and our language testifies to that belief by containing terms which refer to these experiences.

But language does more—much more—in this area of our communications. It enables us to make a unique type of open statement whose meaning depends on our belief that some forms of subjective experience are *universally* disagreeable—or disliked or unpleasant—and that others are *universally* agreeable —or liked or pleasant. For we believe, or we take it for granted, that besides immediate pain, such experiences as fear and frustration are universally disagreeable, and that the sense of physical well-being, confidence, and the ability to *do* what we *want* to do are universally agreeable. This body of ideas, so much a part of our human thinking that it usually passes unnoticed, I call 'the basic-values assumption'. The strongest evidence for the existence of the basic-values assumption is in language: it is shown in the way we speak of things and events according to whether we think they are such as to promote agreeable, or disagreeable, experience. And the way that we speak of them in this connection is *evaluatively*.

See, first, how this applies to the value statement about the apple. On the broad assumption that we all like our needs to be satisfied, the statement that the apple is a good one is equivalent to saying that it is such as to give (the agreeable experience of) *satisfaction* to anyone who has need of an apple.

And notice that on this interpretation the value statement about the apple is informative and impersonal (and therefore debatable). It makes no difference to the meaning of the statement that the apple is good whether the speaker himself has any use for it at all—whether he ever even touches an apple. For the statement, *qua* statement, is not about how the apple affects his emotions or his system of ideals, any more than if he had said it was a red apple; but refers directly to the apple, by asserting in effect that it is *such as to give satis-faction*. In other words, he is saying that it is a satisfactory apple; and 'good' in this type of context is normally equivalent to 'satisfactory'. The contradiction of the statement would be, simply, that the apple is *not* good, or *not* satisfactory: no more and no less. All objects that are understood to have a special use or function are subject to evaluation in these terms, and practical decisions are constantly being made on the basis of this kind of evaluative assessment.

7

However, it is not the case, as Herbert Spencer tried to maintain, that *all* value statements are to be understood ultimately in terms of the servicability or otherwise of objects having particular uses. Even if we leave ethical value statements out of the reckoning this is an over-simplification, seeing that user-satisfaction is not the only emotive experience that human beings are by human beings universally assumed to find agreeable, and its opposite, disagreeable. The basic-values assumption is broader than that. And at this point it seems appropriate to invoke the very broad basic-value concepts of *beneficence, counter-beneficence,* and *harmfulness*.

It is true that we speak much more often of goodness and badness than of beneficence and harmfulness, and that 'counter-beneficence' is a term I have been obliged to invent; but in the prevailing confusion about the use and meaning of value statements the advantage of having these 'blanket' value terms to hand is very considerable, if we take them to cover all the various kinds of goodness, anti-goodness, and badness that may be asserted in open (non-ethical) communications. According to this classification, which, for the sake of convenience, I now

c

adopt, *satisfactoriness* is *one form* of beneficence in the object, but by no means the only one it may have.

Before I go on to elaborate these points it will be as well, at this stage, to summarize what I take to be the chief distinguishing feature of *basic evaluation*, i.e. that kind which (I claim) derives its significance from the basic-values assumption. This can be done for the most part simply by defining its limits.

8

I. No basic-value statement gets its meaning from any belief about the *essential nature* of goodness or of 'the good'; or from any belief or assumption about a 'world of values' corresponding to the world of things.

II. Basic evaluation does not use value terms as expressions of personal liking or aversion, approval or disapproval, etc.

III. My claim of objectivity for basic-value statements does not include the claim that all such statements can be confirmed or falsified by empirical tests, though it does include the claim that some such tests may always be relevant to a discussion or investigation of whether the thing stated to be good or bad really is so in the respect stated (or implied in the context).

IV. Basic-value statements are not ethical statements or judgements. This means that no part of their significance is derived from any conception of the morally right, or of Duty, moral obligation, or what *ought* to be.

V. Basic statements of goodness and badness are not, as they stand, relative statements. If to say that something is good is to say that it is beneficent or has a beneficent tendency this does not *mean* that it is better than something else, or that it approximates to something better than itself.

9

Now, even within the limits set by the conditions laid down above there are *several types* of basic-value statement; so that to ascribe goodness or badness to a thing in these terms is not always to make the same assertion about it. There is nothing particularly awkward about this: we have long been resigned to the fact that there are many kinds of statement whose meaning varies according to context, and I think it will soon appear that the distinction I make between basic-value statements and *all* other classes of value statement is no less sharp because the meanings of the former vary within the limits of their own class.

Before I go on to my analysis of what I call basic-value statements I feel I must apologize in advance for what may well seem an all too familiar 'fuss about words'. Language-analysis is apt to be trivial and boring, and my only excuse for the following exercise in that genre is that I can find no other way of isolating a set of *concepts* which, it appears to me, are badly in need of separation from another set with which they have become snarled up, largely because of what I can only describe as a language situation. I mean the situation in which our value words can stand for various and sometimes incompatible ideas, in contexts which make it difficult for us who use them to determine what we mean by them. For I am not concerned with mutual misunderstandings and cross-purposes in conversation—something which is not, I believe, half so frequent or so important as is apt to be supposed—but with muddled *thinking*, which can be engaged in collectively by means of words, and which seems to be particularly common when values are in question.

So much by way of justification for the brief excursion into the field of language-analysis which follows.

In our open value language I find two main kinds of basic-value statement, each of which may, in its turn, be given (a) a *general*, or (b) a *limited* application. The two main kinds are:

A Statements asserting *particular* beneficence or harmfulness —or contra-beneficence (which I will write as c.-b. for short).

B Statements asserting *comprehensive* beneficence or harmfulness, or c.-b.

A (a). One of the most common forms of value statement is that in which we assert goodness or badness of things we are regarding as means to ends. That this is a special kind of value statement was noted by Aristotle, and the subject has been of interest to axiologists ever since, and has given rise to a lot of theorizing. The problems might have been more easily cleared up if instead of 'What is the nature of this mysterious property of objects of use which we denote by the term "good"?' it had been asked, 'Why do we say "good" when we mean functionally satisfactory?'

Given the basic-values assumption the answer seems clear enough. We say 'good' when we mean functionally satisfactory because we assume that *anyone likes to be able to attain his ends*, whatever they may be. So a 'good' instrument is one which has the beneficent property of giving this kind of *satisfaction*, and the bad instrument has the contra-beneficent property of causing *frustration*. Positively anything which we see as a means to a specific purpose may be called good, quite irrespective of whether it conduces to any sort of agreeable experience at all except user-satisfaction. If nobody has ever been known to refer to a good earthquake or a good hurricane that is only because so far no use has been found for either. But a research worker in a laboratory devoted to developing methods for waging bacteriological warfare could speak quite significantly and informatively of a good disease germ, and support his statement by saying that it is capable of infecting large numbers of people with a fatal disease. If we have reasons for thinking he is mistaken, or is lying, we can say that on the contrary, it is not a good germ. Why not? because it is not reliable— effective measures can very easily be taken against it. Worse still, in the attenuated form in which it is likely to reach the enemy, if at all, it may actually do them good . . . and so on. It would be no contradiction at all of his statement that it is a good germ to say that infecting people with disease harms them, or that disease is always bad because it causes suffering; since, because of the context in which he spoke, he has not said anything to contradict these propositions.

In the case of this type of basic-value statement it is easy to see that the speaker's personal feelings are not implied in the statement. If a military commander reports that the enemy has good aircraft he is certainly not understood to mean that he likes or approves of them.

The value statement which asserts goodness as functional satisfactoriness asserts a *particular* kind of beneficence in the object, and gets its meaning from the assumption that anyone likes to succeed in his aims, whatever they are; and it has *general* application in that when we assert this kind of goodness we are saying that the instrument in question is such as to satisfy not this or that person or group of people, but *anyone* using it for its purpose. The same applies to those other value statements of this class which are about things not directly regarded as means to ends, but which are called, e.g. good as healthful, or bad as dangerous, when we evaluate them by virtue of *one* property on which we are concentrating our attention.

A (b). Not all particular-value statements are of the 'general' type. We may make statements which assert a particular goodness or badness not for 'anyone', but for a group or class, or a single person: e.g., 'Outdoor exercise is good for children'. 'It is bad for poor Mary to have nothing to do but brood over her wrongs'.

It is characteristic of *particular* basic value statements that regarded purely as information they can be expressed in other terms. Instead of saying that an instrument is good we can say that it does efficiently what it is designed to do; and instead of saying that some food or other is good for old people we can say that it keeps them healthy. This being so, one might be inclined to think that it would be perfectly possible to get along without making any value statements of this kind at all, since it seems as if their only practical usefulness lies in their brevity. This view seems to me mistaken. I believe that, on the contrary, our habit of saying 'good' when we mean 'satisfactory' or 'wholesome', and so forth, is of the highest importance. For, to begin with, this usage establishes an essential link between value statements and common-sense statements. One can see a particular-value statement as the evaluative counterpart, so to speak, of a statement about how the object, in being physically as it is, will affect anyone's basic desires in regard to objects of its class. But further, because this particular-value usage is so firmly established, *it provides the material for our statements of comprehensive, general, beneficence, c.-b., and harmfulness.*

B (a). Value statements which assert comprehensive, general, beneficence, c.-b. and harmfulness *cannot* be replaced by statements in any non-evaluative form without losing their special significance. They imply nothing else but value-properties: unique concepts originating in the basic-values assumption. They *can*, however, be reduced back to sets of statements of *particular* value properties, so that we can take them as syntheses of these (though, for a reason to be explained, these syntheses exclude 'satisfactoriness'-evaluations in certain cases). An example will help to bring this out, and also to illustrate the part which statements of comprehensive, general goodness and badness play in our open communications.

Imagine some naturalists debating the proposition that the badger is a preponderantly bad animal: an animal that on balance does more harm than good. They put forward arguments on each side—badgers kill poultry, but they eat harmful insects; they damage the ground by burrowing, but they prey upon the destructive wild rabbit, and so on. None of these statements about the badger's way of life will be equivalent to the proposition being discussed, nor to its opposite. Nor will any one of them as it stands amount to saying 'The badger is bad' (or good) in one way.' And even if it had been possible to assemble every scrap of available information about the ways of badgers as they affect the life of men no summary of it would amount to the statement 'The badger is a preponderantly good animal' or to its opposite.

Yet the fact is that after collecting and weighing various data we do reach just such evaluative conclusions, and act on them. And I think the reason why we are able to do this is clearly because we are in the habit of 'distilling', as it were, *particular-value* statements from statements of any physical conditions which we see as affecting human beings adversely or favourably. It is this which enables us to make the *comprehensive* assessment. The statement 'Badgers kill poultry' implies that badgers interfere with our food-supplies, and because of the basic assumptions that we all dislike being frustrated, and like having enough food, we make the *evaluative substitution* 'Badgers do (one sort of) harm'. And in the same way, 'Badgers eat insects that eat crops' yields, 'Badgers do (one sort of) good'.

(Notice also that in order to be as thorough as possible a comprehensive evaluation should cover, besides whatever affects our material concerns, any features more direct in their influence on human emotions—aesthetic features, for example, may be relevant. In the case of the badgers the pleasure and interest they give to lovers of wild animals should go into the balance along with the other 'pro' considerations.) So when the experts have assembled all that they know about badgers as they affect human interests they will be in a position to make a comprehensive value statement about them based on the known sum of their various particular kinds of goodness and badness. Thus on the basis of the basic-values assumption those statements of *particular* goodness and badness in objects, which for practical purposes can just as well be expressed in terms of their effects, become components of statements of *comprehensive* goodness and badness which can *not* be expressed in any other language than that of evaluation.

Comprehensive evaluation is most variously used. It can be applied, for instance, to a man. We may say a man is good, or bad, meaning that he had a preponderantly beneficent, or harmful, tendency; or at least as often, perhaps, we should say that he has a good or a bad character, meaning that he is in a general way benevolent or malevolent: that his normal propensity is mainly to benefit, or to harm, his fellow-men. Especially when we try to evaluate the characters of historical. figures a great deal of evidence may be aduced on either side, as in the controversies which have raged through centuries over the characters of Richard III and Elizabeth I.[1]

Comprehensive evaluation is also commonly applied to such highly abstract things as past events, trends, discoveries and, so forth; and one might be inclined to wonder what purpose is served by our telling each other that something which has irrevocably happened was either a good or a bad thing. I should

---

[1] Human goodness and badness are often called *moral* goodness and badness, and if 'moral' always only meant something like 'dispositional' there would be no confusion. But unfortunately 'moral' is also used with that entirely different connotation which links it to ethical ideas and ideals. One result of this double-talk is that the concepts of human goodness and badness are often completely divorced from the goodness and badness which may belong to other things. Even more unfortunately 'moral' goodness and badness are discussed in terms which make use of value words *both* in their moral *and* in their non-moral senses indiscriminately, a habit which is very largely responsible for that great tangle of muddled reasoning and ambiguous discourse which I call Moralism.

say that these judgements have the far from trivial function of
helping us to decide what *future* events, as we envisage them,
would be beneficent or harmful on the whole. For one way of
viewing man's past history is to see it as a series of events,
including actions, which have in various degrees and respects
harmed and benefited human beings, and our assessment of
events in these terms is the *only* basis we have on which to
form expectations about the beneficence or harmfulness of
what may happen in the future.

Of course there is no denying that comprehensive evaluation
is fraught with all manner of difficulties and uncertainties.
For in the first place, we cannot possibly take into account
everything that we know quite well to be relevant; and in
the second place there is the fact of our awareness that over
the whole area of human fortunes the account is never closed.
We know that what we now judge to have been a good development at one period may have consequences which will make
us revise our judgement later on; so that in order to reach
any decision we have to set an arbitrary term to our inquiry.
Yet in spite of these difficulties such matters are continually
being thought and talked about, until by the light of what
we know, or hope we know, about the changing needs and
tastes and tendencies of various sorts of people we form opinions
on what would be for the best in basic terms. So those whose
business it is to design policies and institutions intended to
promote or safeguard the happiness of men, or reduce their
unhappiness, are guided by what they believe to have been the
good and bad effects of what was done by their predecessors.
(Often, of course, policies and institutions are not designed to
promote the happiness of anybody but the designers themselves, but that is a different matter.)

B (b). Though we commonly assert comprehensive benefit
and harm as accruing to people in a general way, we may also
assert them in a *limited* sense as accruing to only one person
or group. We say that this or that course of action or event
e.g., will be for the good of—meaning the comprehensive benefit
of—this or that person or group (regardless of any harm that
it may cause to others).

·   ·   ·   ·   ·

I have still to mention a type of value statement which does not fit into any of the classes above, but which nevertheless does seem to derive all its significance from the basic-values assumption. (For convenience I shall only refer to assertions of goodness, but obviously the anaylsis applies equally to their opposites.) This is the sort of statement which asserts a limited goodness—a goodness-for—not as beneficence, but as *conduciveness to* it. We make this sort of statement about agencies affecting things we are considering as means to ends: as when we say that the rain was good for our cabbages. This kind of statement might seem hardly worth mentioning—just an unimportant accident of usage—and so it is, if it is not a statement of goodness-for *live beings regarded as means to ends*. In this case there may be very serious ambiguity. For here we make statements in the form we use for asserting that the thing promotes benefit to *those named in the statement*, when in fact we don't mean to assert anything of the sort. For instance, Cato might have advanced the proposition that frequent beating is good for slaves, meaning purely that this treatment promotes their efficiency as slaves. In this example the meaning is perfectly plain, but it is easy to think of cases where it is not at all clear which sense is intended—cases, for example, of statements about what is good or bad for children, or for animals; and where we may suspect that the speaker is not even clear in his own mind as to what he means. The only way to find out in such cases may be simply to ask him to explain —as, does he mean to say that whatever-it-is tends to benefit these people, or that, via its effects on them, it tends to benefit *us*?

10

This completes my summary of what I take to be the main distinguishable sorts of open value statement that we make in our everyday communications and advance as arguable, or testable, propositions.

By my definition the field for all research into questions of *beneficence* and *harmfulness* is bounded by the *basic-values assumption*, which is implicit in every judgement, every conflict of opinion, and every argument adduced, on this subject. Unless we had the habit of assuming that there are certain

basic emotional experiences and states which, however various may be their external causes, are similarly experience-
able by 'Anyone'—that conceptual 'normal person'—there
could be no words to convey ideas of human benefit
and harm. Unless we assumed that Anyone dislikes the experiences and states we identify by such irreducible terms as
pain, frustration, and anxiety, and likes the experience of
relief from them, and likes their 'positive' opposites, we should
have no grounds for asserting beneficence or harmfulness in
events or actions or anything at all.

II

There are at least two objections which might be advanced on
logical grounds, against my account of basic-value statements.

   The first objection is that if there are allowed to be various
different forms of basic goodness and badness, because there
are various different kinds of basic experience which we severally
regard as universally agreeable and disagreeable, it is possible
to say that one and the same thing is at one and the same time
both good and bad : good as conducive to one sort of experience
and bad as conducive to another. This outrages a long axio-
logical tradition mainly due to Plato, which is still upheld today.[1]
The objection may be expressed by saying that since goodness
and badness are opposite concepts, it is logically impossible
for a thing to be both good and bad.

   One answer to this is to repeat that I have not been trying
to formulate a theory about the *nature* of the good and the bad,
but only to interpret the open statements in which we assert
goodness and badness so as to find out what these statements
have in common, and what they are understood to mean. It
is a fact that we do quite normally say that something is good
in one way and bad in another, and that we justify this by
referring to the effects we expect the thing to have. But in any
case, there is nothing illogical about the statement that a thing
is both good and bad if the properties on account of which
we assert goodness and badness are of different kinds, each

---

[1] 'Well, "the good, that which is good" must therefore be the substantive to
which the adjective ("good") will apply; it must be the whole of that to which the
adjective will apply, and the adjective must *always* truly apply to it.' *Principia
Ethica*, p. 9. Moore.

having its opposite—as, e.g. inefficiency is the opposite of efficiency. It would be illogical to say that a thing is both good because efficient but bad because inefficient, or good because wholesome but bad because unwholesome; but it would not be at all illogical to say that something is good as conducive to immediate pleasure but bad because unwholesome.

A second possible objection relates to our assertions of goodness as conduciveness to user-satisfaction. These are supposed to present a special problem because, as I pointed out above, the ends which the thing is meant to serve may be bad (i.e. harmful or c.-b.). They may be bad in one or in many of the possible ways in which a thing may be bad, and the problem of interpretation is thought to lie in the fact that just in proportion as the ends for which the instrument is designed are bad, its goodness as satisfactoriness for the user is a means to harm. This, however, is really only awkward if we try to understand *this* goodness as a kind which must be added to the sum total of value that a thing has. But there is no need to understand it like this. Efficiency is always a cause of satisfaction to the user, whatever he wants to do; and that is why we so confidently call the efficient thing good—it promotes *one* kind of universally agreeable experience. But clearly, if the purpose is bad, the particular goodness resulting from efficiency must be harmful in the wider field lying outside that of user-satisfaction. The efficiency-goodness is not obliterated by the wider badness, but the being-good in this one way adds to the being-bad in another. Thus in a 'comprehensive' evaluation (see Section 9, B(a)) if the property of giving user-satisfaction forms part of the assessment we shall naturally only include it on the 'pro' side if and when we have reached an otherwise favourable verdict.

12

A certain state of affairs must prevail, however, to produce this conflict between efficiency-goodness and other kinds. It is, precisely, the state of affairs in which *human interests conflict*. In the absence of conflict of interests the good instrument would do no harm; it would serve its user's purpose without injury to anybody else.

(Conflict of interests has some relevance to this discussion because in terms of basic evaluation we can show that, openly speaking, conflict of interests is comprehensively bad—harmful. As follows. An event which benefits one person and does no harm to anyone else is universally beneficent—humanity is 'one up' because of it. But if in benefiting one person an event does an equal amount of harm to another it is not universally beneficent. If we imagine the whole of humanity neatly divided into two mutually hostile camps, with interests so sompletely at variance that what was good for one group was in precisely the same degree bad for the other there could be no such thing as a universally beneficent event at all. Short of this, wherever there is conflict the extent of possible general benefit is restricted; so that a situation in which interests conflict is objectively bad to the extent of that conflict. The ideal model of this situation is the state of war. Whatever the scale and scope of the war, unless it is a war of extermination, the essential thing is not that each side is directly trying to kill as many people as possible on the other side. As a rule the killing is only an incidental part of the general policy, which is *to cause as much suffering* as possible to the other side, so as to make them prefer to give in rather than continue the struggle. This is the literally harmful aspect of war; it is what makes war bad in the plain 'open' sense that the main business of each of the parties is to cause as much disliked experience—as much pain, disease, hunger, frustration, fear, and grief as possible to the other.)

13

I hope I have now dealt with the main objections which might be raised against my account of a scheme of evaluation which, I have been arguing, is embodied in our normal work-a-day uses of value terms. But because I realize that it challenges a very widely-favoured view about the nature of all evaluation, I must say a further word about my claim of *objectivity* or *impersonality* of basic evaluation.

Emotional bias may *underlie* any statement, however matter-of-fact. Even that classic example of a bare factual statement 'the cat is on the mat' may be fraught with emotion if the mat happens to be a brand-new white one, and the cat has just come out of the coal-hole. In the same way, you may hear it said that a thing is good or is bad in a tone of voice expressing delight, rage, astonishment or what you will; but if the statement belongs to the class of basic evaluations the emotional feelings of the speaker don't add an iota of meaning to the statement *as* a statement. That something, some event, will benefit the whole of mankind might be asserted by a man without one scrap of benevolence in his whole character—it might be said by the Devil himself in a tone of the deepest regret—and *qua* statement it would mean exactly the same as if it came from the lips of the greatest philanthropist who ever lived. *For the content of a value statement is the same no matter how it is uttered or who utters it, if its meaning depends on the basic-values assumption.*

14

Basic evaluation yields no certainties. Nor am I claiming that it is the only consistent, or logical, or 'true' kind of evaluation. All I claim for it is that it can be consistently and significantly applied to anything that we see as influencing the fortunes of human beings; that it can be applied to such various things as tools, food, people, and behaviour; to governments and policies; to religions, and even to philosophies in so far as they affect human interests and aims. I claim also that basic evaluation can be applied to *actions* as they affect other people: the good action *benefits*, the bad action *harms*; and that intentions as well, even though we only infer them, can be asserted to be good or bad, still in the objective sense, meaning that the agent's intention was to do good or to do harm (matters on which judges and juries often have to reach decisions, on whatever evidence is available). In short, I claim for basic evaluation that it is a convenient tool for the evaluative handling of anything that concerns us, and that theoretically speaking nothing that affects our human interests is too large or too small or too elusive for it to grasp.

15

The particular consequence of the above claim that I want to urge here is that *in basic evaluation we have the means for evaluating, among other things, those values and systems of evaluation that are called* ethical.

But even assuming that this critical exercise is possible in theory, haven't, in fact, the two kinds of values become so closely intertwined, both in moral philosophy and in the ideas of laymen, that it is virtually impossible to separate them?

It is my belief that the disentangling can still be done—on one condition: that, following Kant, we recognize *Duty* as the cardinal ethical concept from which all the rest—the moral *Ought*, *Right*, and *Wrong*, and the moral *Good* and *Bad* derive that peculiar and altogether distinct sort of authority that they traditionally boast. So in the next chapter I shall argue that if we isolate the element of moral exhortation, the 'It is your Duty . . .' we shall have arrived at what is, beyond dispute, the *purely ethical* core of any 'moral system'. If I can establish this, it will afterwards be a fairly simple matter to decide what kind of values belong properly to Ethics, and what kind are none of its business.

3

DESCRIPTION, ADVICE,
AND EXHORTATION

> *Whoever prescribes to another what actions he must
> perform or omit if he wishes to further his own happiness,
> might perhaps be able to bring all doctrines of morality
> under this requirement. But then these prescriptions are
> no longer obligations, but merely directions for behaviour
> suitable to achieving an end.*
>
> KANT.

SUMMARY: What is the essential characteristic of an ethical system? Aristotle's *Ethics* in so far as it is devoted to
description of the 'noble' man's way of life, or to *advice* to
those in pursuit of happiness, lacks the distinctive feature
of pure Ethics, namely a basis in the idea of Duty or an
an absolute Ought. I show, however, that Aristotle does
introduce this concept in his observations on Nature's
ideal for man, which include an implicit exhortation to
fulfil it as a Duty; so the *Ethics* has, in fact, the characteristic stamp of pure Ethics. I argue that without this
basis in the notion of a transcendent Duty Ethics
degenerate into *Moralism* (analysed and discussed in the
chapter following), thereby corrupting both ethical
values and basic (non-ethical) values.

I

Moral philosophers have never been able to reach a satisfactory
measure of agreement among themselves on what is the proper
subject-matter of ethical theory. Some cast their net so wide
as to cover every sort of judgement expressing approval or
preference, and every choice between alternatives, as well as
every consistently held principle of conduct—whether adopted
for reasons of general expediency, or because it is Right

according to some purely moral standard. Often an ethical theorist will almost entirely neglect concepts which some fellow-theorist regards as crucial, though possibly without going out of his way to reject them in so many words. For instance, Bentham and his disciples ignore the idea of Perfection, which is the central ethical preoccupation of the Christian Platonists.

There are two main kinds of problem in ethical theory. One kind belongs to the department of language-analysis, and deals in such questions as, what is the significance and the scope of the word 'ought'?. The other kind of problem has to do with practice, and leads to inquiries into the principles which determine what Ought to be done, or into what principles Ought to determine what Ought to be done. But in fact, the two kinds of problem are seldom kept apart for long, because whoever writes about these matters on the assumption that 'ought' and the value-words are 'moral' words is almost sure to start with certain preconceptions about the essential nature of the moral motive or moral action, so that what may have begun as an objective study sooner or later becomes ethically dogmatic.

2

Sidgwick, for instance, was among those who believed that the sense of moral obligation must be intuitively given, and because he was himself convinced that our supreme obligation is to promote human happiness or to produce the greatest possible net balance of human good, he tried to show that his own conviction must be universally shared. It is endearingly characteristic of Sidgwick that because he was so sure that the concept of Duty is derived from a sense of obligation to promote the general good, he should have left quite out of account that distinctively ethical idea of Duty which derives from belief in a God whose will must be done *no matter what* he demands. (Think, for example, of Abraham's willingness to sacrifice his own son in obedience to a caprice of Jehovah's.)

3

Professor C. D. Broad's *Five Types of Ethical Theory* brings out very sharply the divergencies between the moral philosophies of Spinoza, Butler, Hume, Kant, and Sidgwick. Spinoza and Hume have, it is pointed out, 'no Categorical Imperative'. That is, they do not deal in the concept of an ultimate criterion of Duty or moral obligation. Neither do they hold that there is any principle of conduct which Ought absolutely to be followed, although they both exhibit a strong bias in favour of humaneness. Butler, Kant, and Sidgwick are true Ethicists, for all their differences. Butler believed in a faculty called Conscience or 'the principle of reflection' which it is man's Duty, as well as his interest, to obey. Kant's moral law is the ultimate criterion for morally Right action, which excludes all interest as a motive. Sidgwick's conception of Duty is based on the intuition that happiness Ought to be promoted.

The views of contemporary moral philosophers are just as various, except that most of them agree that ordinary value language bears closely upon ethical questions, though they still differ as to what the nature of that bearing is. But, by contrast, H. A. Prichard, one of the founders of the school of modern Intuitionism, concentrates on the idea of Moral Obligation, and comes to the conclusion that there are really no moral problems, linguistic or otherwise. We know that what is obligatory is what we know to be obligatory, and that, ultimately, is that. Others, again, uphold a kind of traditionalism in morals. R. M. Hare, for instance, finds the source of Right conduct in principles founded on traditions and social conventions which have stood the test of time, though he also insists that the individual's own judgement must have the last word in moral decisions.

4

Among present-day philosophers A. C. Ewing takes an unusually comprehensive view of the scope of Ethics. He ranks all acts of choice impartially as ethical or moral, and apparently regards *every* taste and preference as an ethical attitude of mind. Thus he writes:

> The position of the absolute ethical sceptic is analogous to that of the absolute theoretical sceptic . . . just as the theoretical sceptic can still talk, so the ethical sceptic can still act in accordance with his desires, but he cannot consistently claim

D

that there is any justification for any of his acts; that any one
is more rational than any other.[1]

The statement that the ethical sceptic cannot claim that any
of his acts is justified, or is more rational than any other only
makes sense on the assumption that all justifications are ethical
justifications, and all reasons ethical reasons. It seems probable,
however, that the key 'ethical' concept here is that of *value*;
for continuing in the same context Dr. Ewing writes (p. 33
op. cit.):

> The sceptic as to values is not entitled to believe even the
> proposition that it is more reasonable to wash his hands in
> water than in sulphuric acid, for this presupposes at any rate
> that pain is evil. So he has no real ground for not washing his
> hands in sulphuric acid. To say that he does not like to do so
> is to give a psychological cause and not a reason, unless we
> assume that it is *good* to do what one likes or that our desires
> ought to be satisfied.

The argument seems to be that since every choice is based
on an evaluation, and all evaluation is ethical, every act of
choice, which is to say every intentional act, is done because
of the belief that it is *good* to do it, and that no other reason
can be found. Such an all-embracing view of the scope of
Ethics is rarely stated, but it does reflect a characteristic new
trend in modern ethical theory. In the past the great majority
of moral philosophers were chiefly interested in principles of
action to be applied in the relations between man and man,
or between man and God, and seldom tried to prove that a
set of opinions about what it is *good* to do provided our only
reasons for acting with ordinary sanity.

5

Any random sampling of the vast literature of Ethics shows
how difficult it is to decide just what ethical theory is, and is
not, about. Is its main business to inquire into the current
beliefs, tastes, and conduct-conventions of a particular culture
—the investigator's own? Nearly all moral philosophers deal
to a large extent with this subject, but it is also the proper study

[1] *The Definition of Good*, pp. 32–33.

of sociologists. Or is it the business of ethical theory to examine and classify the various motives which underlie our voluntary actions? Ethicists from Aristotle to Kant and onwards to G. E. Moore and his followers have given a great deal of attention to this subject, but nowadays it is systematized under the heading of psychology. Does ethical theory examine by the light of (a) linguistic analysis or (b) recorded intuitive feelings, or both, the significance of the words Ought, Duty, and Moral Obligation? This is often treated as the main concern of ethical analysis; yet it is covered by the two disciplines of linguistics and psychology. It seems best, then, to say that whatever the distinguishing feature of Ethics or ethical theory may be, it is not to be found in the subjects which fall within its scope, but rather in the way that it handles them.

Even so, it might seem reasonable to limit the range of Ethics so far as to exclude any studies in which values are simply irrelevant, though what studies this actually does exclude remains a debatable matter. By Dr. Ewing's interpretation even the exact sciences, in that they emerged as distinct subjects through people choosing to concentrate on one thing rather than another, are ethical in origin, and are carried on by those who, being engaged in choosing theories to work on, choosing methods of research, choosing to use what they find relevant and discarding what they don't, all move about their laboratories in response to ethical stimuli. Still, even Dr. Ewing would presumably allow that ethical theory has nothing to say about the data of physics *as such*.

So perhaps at this stage we had better say with deliberate vagueness that Ethics has to do with men's purposes and their purposive acts. This being settled we can go on to examine what is distinctive about the ethical approach, so that if possible we can, at least in some cases, say definitely, '*This* way of looking at the matter is ethical; *this* way is not.'

6

Aristotle's *Ethics*, the prototype of systematized ethical theory, is the most obvious source from which to seek enlightenment on the question of what Ethics distinctively is.

Aristotle surveyed his own culture through the spectacles of

an educated member of a small privileged class; which is to
say that, as educated, he viewed it with some measure of critical
detachment, and as privileged, approved of it on the whole
and wanted it to be preserved. The *Ethics* was written by way
of prolegomena to the *Politics*, but actually it contains much
which is not directly relevant to the business of formulating
principles of legislation for the community at large, matters
with which the *Politics* proper deals.

Aristotle first carefully analyses the concept of goodness,
distinguishing between the things and activities which are
valued because they are means to further good, and the goodness which for man is ultimate, namely happiness, which, he
says, is the end beyond which we cannot desire anything, since
happiness itself is the chief good, and is that for the sake of
which everything else is done.

The material on which Aristotle based his conclusions came
from his observations of what things were in fact sought, prized,
and admired; and he constantly refers to current opinion and
current usage, remarking that the matters he is treating of
do not admit of exact proofs and demonstrations. He invokes
human judgement and opinion in support of his conclusion
that the highest happiness is to be found in a life devoted to
reasoning and contemplation. Thus many of his conclusions
are based on *description*: their force depends on an account of
what Aristotle sees as the actual situation as regards human
tastes and needs. (According to Aristotle, however, the *common*
man's interests were not of much account except as they might
affect social stability, for although he was capable of feeling
pleasure of a sort he could know nothing of true happiness.
'The many are plainly quite slavish, choosing a life like that of
the brutes.' Aristotle remarks, and he also says of them that
they can have no idea of 'what is truly noble and pleasant'.[1]

7

Now so long as Aristotle is treating of what he has noticed about
human nature, or drawing inferences, from his observations,
as to what is 'valued' or held to be good, he is simply recording

[1] For the quotations I have used Peters's translation of the *Ethics*.

facts as he sees them, or making guesses. He is writing in the character of an observer and interpreter. This is not 'Ethics' according to any view which differentiates it from the business of noting and interpreting an aspect of human behaviour. The fact that the investigator's own tastes and preferences are rather obtrusive and lead now and then to distortions only impairs the usefulness of his information and his deductions, it does not alter the nature of the study itself.

8

Aristotle, however, was out to do more than investigate and describe: his main purpose was to advise. (That he chose often to write in the language of description rather than of direct advice, saying, 'The noble man does this', instead of, 'You must do this so as to be a truly noble man', is immaterial. The obvious intention in such cases is to recommend one sort of conduct and deprecate the other.)

Advice is an entirely different sort of utterance from description or analysis, and its purpose is to influence actions; so we may consider whether it is the fact that the *Ethics* consists largely of advice which makes it what we should nowadays call 'ethical'.

The difficulty is, however, that there are some sorts of advice which hardly anyone calls ethical; for example, the advice which is technical instruction, or any general treatment of how to be proficient is some special field of action. Nobody calls a knitting-leaflet an ethical work, and Mrs. Beeton's treatises on household management and cookery have seldom, I think, been put in that category, neither is her famous maxim 'A place for everything, and everything in its place' taken as a *moral* maxim.

Is this perhaps because her advice (setting aside her pronouncements about the proper relations between mistress and servants), is not on the treatment of people, but of inanimate objects such as saucepans and table-linen?

On reflection it does not seem as if this could be the whole story, at least if it implies that any advice on how to treat people *is* ethical. Perhaps we might feel that Aristotle's recommendations to the noble man on how to behave towards his equals (haughtily), and his inferiors (affably), has something ethical about it, but if this were purely *because* it concerns the treatment of others the advice in *How to Win Friends and Influence People*—a work, incidentally, of monumental ruthlessness and cynicism—must be ethical too, as well as any other manual of instructions for dealing with human beings: a handbook for drill-sergeants, for example, if there is such a thing.

Possibly the reason why the types of advice I have just instanced do not seem to meet the requirements for being ethical in the most acceptable sense of the term is that they are of the sort offered to people who want to attain some particular *kind* of proficiency; that they are only relevant to some strictly limited field of action.

Aristotle's advice, by contrast, is general. He offers his *élite* certain principles to follow in the whole conduct of their lives— notably the principle of avoiding both excess and insufficiency.

Is this, then, the necessary condition for ethical advice—that it must lay down one or more principles for living, or a general scheme for conduct to apply in all or most situations where one has a choice of action?

Such principles might, of course, be entirely self-centred. The advice may be good advice, but good only for the advisee himself. On this interpretation therefore a treatise entitled *How to be Happy Through Making Other People Miserable* might be an impeccably ethical work. And indeed, if to live under strict control by laws applying to every department of life is to be miserable, we might on a one-sided interpretation of Aristotle's doctrines give this title to a fair portion of the *Ethics*. It depends a good deal on one's point of view.

Anyhow, we are now confronting a conception of Ethics to which the notion of doing good to anyone but oneself is irrelevant.

Perhaps, though, we could mend matters by adding the qualification that whilst not all advice on general principles for living is ethical, advice on general principles for living such that to conform to the principles would tend to make one act beneficently or in socially desirable ways would be ethical. On this view 'Honesty is the best policy' would be ethical advice, and 'Always look to the main chance' would not be.

9

But now, when at last we seem to have arrived at a conception of ethicalness which seems to agree fairly well with the popular view of it, we find that the notion of *advice*, which we took first to be the distinguishing feature of that part of the *Ethics* which is not quite obviously non-ethical, begins to slip through our fingers. For as advice such a saying as 'Always be honest' can have no greater authority over our actions than 'Always be shrewd'; we shall have no more reason to follow the former than the latter unless we believe that honesty is, from our own point of view, the best policy.

This is perhaps the crux of the matter, for we seem here to have found at least one distinguishing characteristic of ethical utterances: that they appear to make some very special sort of claim on us *over and above* any claim to further our ends or advance our interests. What is the exact nature of that claim it may be hard to decide, but if this element really is present in all ethical utterances then *no type of advice is ethical at all*.

For what is typical of advice is, of course, that it is offered on the stated or unstated assumption that the person to whom it is addressed has some specific end in view that the advice will help him to realize. The end may be as narrow as sowing a row of peas, or as broad as saving civilization—it is all the same; for the significance of advice lies only in the adviser's assumption of *an end in view*. (This is just what distinguishes a piece of advice from an *exhortation*, which is not tied to the idea of an end.) Advice, in fact, can always be formulated as follows: 'If you want to achieve this, you ought to do that.'

As advice, therefore, such an utterance as 'You ought to be kind to your neighbour' must be backed by the understanding that the person addressed has some end in view that being kind to his neighbour may help him to realize. (Otherwise it is not advice at all, but *exhortation*.)

Now Aristotle assumed that those whom he was addressing in the *Ethics* had all one constant, ultimate end in view, namely *to attain happiness*. This he expressed by saying that happiness was the chief good. So the advice he offered them was directed to helping them to attain to the state of happiness and continue in it. Thus like all advice his could be expressed according to

the formula, 'If you want . . . then you ought . . . ' and every
piece of advice in the *Ethics* is to be taken as prefaced by an
implicit 'If you want happiness'. For this reason it was not
necessary for Aristotle to draw any distinction between the
ethical and the non-ethical in the recommendations he made
to his readers. No matter what sort of activity he was recommending, or what principles of conduct, all those of his words
which are in the form of advice are made to a group of people
aiming always at happiness.

10

It is Aristotle's assumption that happiness is and must be the
end of all rationally directed human endeavour which has led
many critics to deny that the *Ethics* is really 'ethical', or to
deny, at the very least, that it is 'in the highest sense' ethical;
which criticism at any rate means—whatever it may mean in
addition—that the *Ethics* does not embody what they see as
that quintessential something which makes Ethics what it
uniquely is.

This sense of the insufficiency of the *Ethics* is typically
expressed by J. A. Smith in his Introduction to the Everyman
Edition of the work called *The Ethics of Aristotle*. Commenting
on Aristotle's notion of man's 'supreme good' he says,

> But this end is not conceived as presented to him by a superior
> power, nor even as something which *ought* to be. The presenta-
> tion of the Moral Ideal as Duty is almost absent. From the out-
> set it is identified with the object of desire, or what we not
> merely judge desirable but actually do desire, or that which
> would, if realized, satisfy human desire.

Further on he remarks:

> [In] Aristotle's Moral Philosophy . . . the end is the enjoyment
> of Happiness, not the fulfilment of Duty . . . Every human prac-
> tical activity derives its value from its efficiency as a means to
> that end; it is good or bad, right or wrong, as it conduces, or
> fails to conduce, to happiness.

11

Dr. Smith seems, however, to have missed a theme in the *Ethics*
which makes it not so entirely amoral as he thinks. 'The end
is the enjoyment of Happiness', he says quite justly, but when
he adds to this '—and not the fulfilment of Duty', he discounts
a part of Aristotle's argument which is no less significant and
important because it cannot be altogether reconciled with the
premise about happiness. For whilst it is true that Aristotle
declares happiness to be the end of all human endeavour, he
introduces, in scattered observations here and there, the concept of something which is more like an ideal to be lived up
to, than a desire to be realized.

The word 'ἀρετή, translated as 'virtue', occurs very often in
the *Ethics*, and in most cases it seems to mean merely the collec-
tion of attributes in a man which the good or noble man
approves and puts into practice; for instance courage, integrity,
and self-control, all of which are shown to conduce to his own
happiness in the long run. But it very soon transpires that by
the *good* man Aristotle means not only, or even mainly, the
man who benefits other men, but rather he who does what is
most suited to his status as a human being; and the best possible sort
of man is he who finds his happiness in devoting his life to
contemplation. So it is in the region of his remarks about
human goodness, rather than about virtue, that we find the
strongest suggestion of a criterion of value outside, or over and
above, the felicific one.

12

A dichotomy in the notion of goodness has in fact already
begun to emerge in Aristotle's discussion of the nature of
happiness itself, where happiness is associated with the life of
reason. If, as he argues, happiness is the end of all endeavour,
and everything which is good is so by virtue of being a means
to it, one would conclude that this superiority of one sort of
activity over any other sort must be simply due to its being
likely to promote the agent's happiness more effectively. Yet
there are hints that some other consideration is involved as
well.

The following passage comes in Chapter VII of Book I immediately after Aristotle has first laid down his happiness-principle:

> What is the function of man? For as the goodness and the excellence of a piper or a sculptor or the practiser of any art, and generally of those who have any function or business to do, lies in that function, so man's good would seem to lie in his function, if he has one. But can it be supposed that whilst a carpenter and a cobbler have a function and a business of their own, man has no business and no function assigned to him by Nature? Nay, surely as his several members, eye and hand and foot, plainly each have its own function, so we must suppose that man also has some function over and above all these.

The argument is from analogy. If other things have their proper functions Man must have his, and if men practising certain skills can excel in these, so too can Man *as* Man, in *his* special function, which is to exercise his soul in reasoning and contemplation. Here something which was barely hinted at in the analysis of the means to happiness is now made explicit, and Aristotle emerges as the exponent of a purely metaphysical conception of the Best sort of life for the Best sort of man. If anyone should raise the question of *why* man should choose to fulfil the function that Nature has assigned to him the reply might well be that there is no 'why' about it; for in this, as in everything else, what Nature decrees is simply what happens according to Nature's own laws; but this, one feels, is not the answer Aristotle would have given. He writes, rather, like Nature's *advocate*, urging her creature Man in exalted language to carry out her purposes and speaking now with the true voice of moral exhortation—Man *ought* to fulfil his proper function. That he will be happy in so doing is a fact, says Aristotle; but the reason why he ought to do so is that this *is* his proper function—that it is *right*, that it is his Duty to Nature, to do so. Therefore I should say that the *Ethics* does contain the germ of what has continued to be most characteristic of ethical doctrine to this day: the idea of an ultimate human Duty which is laid down not by men, but by some authoritative Principle dwelling above and beyond all human desires, and superior to any of them.

13

Aristotle's treatise anticipates later developments in moral theory in another respect too. It is the prototype, in fact, of that kind of moral exposition that moves to and fro across the borderline between pure Ethics and ideas of value which are not ethical at all in any strict sense. For although he introduces a conception of rightness and goodness which is discernibly different from the rightness and goodness which concerns men in their everyday activities and aims, and although the goodness of the means to any given end is differentiated from that of the end which is ultimate,[1] *no clear distinction* is ever drawn between the goodness which derives from avowedly human standards unrelated to anything beyond human concerns, and that Goodness which is attached to the notion of the absolute and transcendent. The result of this ambiguity is that the word 'good' itself is used ambiguously—particularly when applied to men and their actions—blurring the distinction between Higher values and human ones.

14

I have looked at the *Ethics* in order to see whether it contains anything which cannot be placed under the heading either of *description* or of *advice*, and which is directed to influencing conduct, and I conclude that only the observations about the 'function' of man and the implied exhortation to fulfil it as a Duty have this exclusive, distinctive character, and that this part of the *Ethics* alone, therefore, is entitled to be called purely ethical.

Admittedly there are very many moral philosophers who would not agree to this restriction of the scope of the 'ethical', which they would make much wider: wide enough at the very least to accommodate various kinds of *advice*. But my justification, apart from the authority of Kant, for excluding advice

---

[1] . . . but those things which are pursued and loved on their own account, are predicated under one species, whilst the things which produce these, or in any way preserve them, or prevent the contrary, are said to be goods on account of these, and after another manner. It is evident, then, that goods may be so called in two ways; some on their own account, the others on account of the former.' Book I. Ch. VI.

from the 'ethical' category is, firstly, that it seems impossible
to draw any line of demarcation between advice which some
would call ethical, and advice which hardly anyone would call
ethical—e.g. technical instruction—and secondly, and more
decisively, that advice is not a type of utterance which owes
anything at all to the idea of Duty or the unconditioned Ought,
which are by general consent peculiar to Ethics, and which
certainly a majority of Ethicists—as distinct from ethical
theorists—take to be the key concepts of any ethical system
worthy of the name. If therefore we are to draw any distinction
between ethical and non-ethical suasive utterances it seems
legitimate to draw it here, at the point where *advice* gives place
to *exhortation*. And I believe this is the only point at which it is
possible to draw a dividing-line which does not cross any part
of that moralistic no-man's-land where so many bitter but
inconclusive battles are fought with two-edged words.

(Because the terms 'good', 'right', and 'ought' have different
meanings according to whether they are being used in a context
which is ethical in the above sense or not, I shall from now
on always write them with initial capitals when referring to
their use in ethical senses.)

4

ETHICS AND MORALISM

> *For it is the peculiarity of ethical legislation to perform*
> *actions solely because they are Duties, and to make the*
> *principle of Duty itself the adequate spring of the will,*
> *no matter whence the Duty may be derived.*
>
> KANT.
>
> *If anyone asks us, 'Why ought I to do these acts you call*
> *my duty?' the only answer is, 'Because they are your duty',*
> *and if he does not see this we cannot make him.*
>
> E. F. CARRITT.

SUMMARY: 'The problem which delimits the field of Ethics is not that of the empirically good and valuable, but that of the right and morally imperative', writes C. I. Lewis. Much confusion results from the failure to recognize the force of this distinction. Accepting it, I go on to argue for the (Kantian) view that what is 'right and morally imperative' must ultimately be determined by *the individual sense of Duty*, and therefore that there can be *no universal ethical values* and only one *universal ethical principle*, namely, 'It is your Duty to obey your sense of Duty' —which is a truism, but which might function effectively as an *exhortation*. Many attempts have been made to formulate systems which will dissolve the distinction between *ethical* and *basic* evaluation—e.g. by equating ethically-determined 'Goodness'—which is moral rectitude in the Kantian sense—with benevolence and beneficence. Such systems, with their consequences for the theory of evaluation, I classify and discuss under the head of *Moralism*.

I

In basic evaluation the idea of goodness is linked to the idea of benefit or advantage, and to assert goodness is to assert actual or potential beneficence.

Purely ethical Goodness, on the other hand, may be completely divorced from beneficence, particularly when attributed to conduct. For ethically Good conduct is conduct conforming to an ethical standard, no matter what that standard may be. Therefore *any* sort of conduct, if only it is conceived to be moral or dutiful, may be Good irrespective of whether benefit is likely to result, or has resulted, or could possibly result, for anybody in the world.

Many moral philosophers have noticed the ambiguities in the use of 'good', but they often tend to underestimate the difficulties which anyone would face who tried to purge his ethical terminology of all non-ethical meanings. Thus C. I. Lewis writes:

> The problem which delimits the field of Ethics is not that of the empirically good or valuable but that of the right and morally imperative. To be sure, there is essential connection between rightness of action and goodness in that which the action is intended to effect . . . But . . . we should be careful that we do not illicitly connect the right and the good before ever we have distinguished them. By an ambiguity of language right acts are also called good acts and those whose acts are right are called good people . . . but 'good' meaning 'useful for conducing to satisfaction' and 'good' meaning Justified or Praiseworthy are two different words, however much this double usage may suggest a connection discerned by the common man.[1]

I shouldn't myself draw the distinction between the two kinds of 'good' just here. 'Good' is not very often used to mean the same as 'justified', though a moralist would probably hold that no act which he called justified could be morally Bad; and 'praiseworthy', though certainly acceptable as a 'moral' term, is less distinctively moral than Right (or Moral). Professor Lewis doesn't attempt to place 'rightness' or 'moral imperativeness' in any logical relationship to goodness-as-usefulness, and he seems almost to admit that he doesn't see how this could be done. The effect of his comment is to remind us how necessary this ambiguity of 'good' often is to give substance to ethical discourse. It is this difference-without-a-distinction which tempts the Moralist to make the best of both worlds by deriving

[1] *An Analysis of Knowledge and Valuation*, p. 555.

his ethical Goodness first from some transcendent idea—saying that that is good which is in conformity with a principle Higher than human desires or aims—and then reinforcing his exhortations to embrace the principle by arguing that it will be good-as-advantageous to do so. In this way non-moral motives are appealed to in order to encourage us to give precedence to moral motives; and ethical 'Good', which connotes Duty, invokes the support of its humbler namesake which connotes benefit. (I shall later give some examples of this, particularly with reference to the Ethics of Kant.)

A similar, though converse, procedure is adopted by Moralists who try to use Duty as a buttress for goodness, taking it for granted that the deliverances of the sense of Duty always direct us to do what is good-as-beneficent. But their 'tacit equation' between Duty or Conscientiousness and goodness is sheer wishful thinking, as has been stressed by Professor Nowell-Smith:

> Many of the worst crimes in history have been committed by men who had a strong sense of duty just because their sense of duty was so strong.[1] (p. 247).

Nowell-Smith refuses to allow that the harm which sometimes results from 'conscientiousness' is merely the outcome of stupidity or miscalculation by the agents:

> May not the harm spring from their very conscientiousness? We might adopt the moral principle that conscientiousness is so valuable that a man ought to be conscientious no matter what harm he does; but it is quite another thing to say that their conscientiousness is never the source of the harm that good men do (p. 248).

It is one of the many merits of this book to remind us that the sense of Duty is not necessary to inspire men to care about their fellows, and further, that moral convictions are not necessary to induce some men to exert themselves to the utmost for the good of others:

> A man can consistently adopt a policy of doing good to others, not because he regards it as his duty, but because that is what he most wants to do and enjoys doing ... But his altruism is not necessarily less consistent or more easily shaken than that of the man who tries to do good because he thinks it his duty (p. 253).

[1] This and the following quotations are taken from P. H. Nowell-Smith, *Ethics*, 1954 (Penguin Books).

2

Among present-day moral philosophers there is a decided leaning towards Moralism; a tendency to widen the scope of Ethics so as to make it embrace both Good and good, using arguments which try to link ordinary goodness to Duty or moral obligation. (This trend, which had already appeared in the Utilitarians, was given a new stimulus by G. E. Moore.) Anyone might have expected that this moralistic movement would have met with strong opposition from the Radical Empiricists or Logical Positivists, who objected to the intrusion of metaphysics into our communications. But what they actually did was to demonstrate very strikingly that they were as much under the influence of the moralistic mode of thought as anybody else, and the effect of their intervention was almost certainly to reinforce it. At first, as though accepting the sweeping claims of such writers as Dr. Ewing (see Chapter 3, section 4) quite naïvely and uncritically, the Logical Positivists treated *all* value statements as equally 'metaphysical'; which meant, in effect, meaningless. R. Carnap, for instance, wrote:

> Actually a value statement is nothing else than a command in a misleading grammatical form. It may have effects upon the actions of men, and these effects may either be in accordance with our wishes or not; but it is neither true nor false.[1]

Thus according to Carnap in those days, all value statements were equally meaningless. The above passage occurs in a paragraph headed ETHICS, and it is highly significant of the power of Moralism that Carnap should have been trapped into making such a false generalization because he identified all value statements with moral exhortations, never having considered the humble claim that they can be *informative*. Wittgenstein also ascribed non-significance to *all* value statements with his dictum, 'If there is a value it must lie outside all happening and being-so.'[2] This, according to his criterion, means that a value statement is not a statement; and we find the same blindness to the significance of value statements in the following from Bertrand Russell:

[1] *Philosophy and Logical Syntax*, p. 24 (London, 1935).
[2] *Tractatus Logico-Philosophicus* 6. 41.

If, now, a philosopher says, 'beauty is good', I may interpret him as meaning either, 'Would that everybody loved the beautiful' . . . or, 'I wish that everybody loved the beautiful', . . . The first of these makes no assertion but expresses a wish; since it affirms nothing, it is logically impossible that there should be evidence for or against it, or for it to possess either truth or falsehood. The second sentence, instead of being merely optative, does make a statement, but it is one about the philosopher's state of mind, and it could only be refuted by evidence that he does not have the wish that he says he has.[1]

The implication of this is that 'Beauty is good' cannot very well mean anything other than 'Would that everybody . . .' or 'I wish that everybody . . .'. But of course this is not so. If we were to interpret it as meaning that beauty, as the characteristic of giving aesthetic pleasure, does little harm to outweigh the pleasure it gives, and so is on balance a beneficent thing, the statement 'Beauty is good' is surely as 'meaningful', and debatable, as any other generalization about the effects of a thing on human beings. Russell, however, as we see, does not reckon with the possibility that the remark could be any sort of *proposition*, and this is because, like Carnap after him, he took the adjective 'good' to connote not benefit but something vaguely 'ethical'. Perhaps if he had chosen for his example some other abstraction than beauty; say religion, or war, or philosophy, he might have found more to say, for in that case he must surely have noticed that the goodness could indicate beneficence, and so be debatable by the light of experience.

You may search in vain through the writings of Russell, Carnap, or Wittgenstein for any treatment of value terms which includes a clear separation of ethical from non-ethical value language. These philosophers do not *argue* that there is no such distinction. They simply take it for granted that none exists: though this was perhaps only to be expected of those already afflicted by the awkwardness of having to recognize more than one kind of meaninglessness.

[1] *Religion and Science* (Butterworth), p. 236–7.

E

3

The non-ethical values have few champions, so it was left to
the Ethicists to protest against the Empiricists' disrespectful
treatment of values—by which the Ethicists meant Values—and
this they most volubly did. In his book entitled *A Critique of
Logical Positivism*, which mainly consisted of a sustained attack
on A. J. Ayer's *Language, Truth, and Logic*, C. E. M. Joad wrote:

> If you destroy the grounds for believing in an objective value,
> you will hold that those who have in fact believed in it have
> been mistaken and that their beliefs have been irrational.
> Among these beliefs are (I) that some human characters and
> some courses of action are *really* better than others; (II) that
> good cannot be equated with what any person or body of
> persons happens to approve of; and (III) that our duty ought
> to be performed however disagreeable it may happen to
> be (p. 144).

And elsewhere he adds,

> Finally, if Logical Positivism is correct you can say, 'One atom
> bomb can destroy 50,000 people' (statement of fact), but not 'It
> is a bad thing to destroy 50,000 people' (statement of evalua-
> tion); or rather, you can say it, but the word 'bad' adds nothing
> to the factual content of the statement (p. 148).

In face of such reproaches it was not long before some
leading Logical Positivists began to feel that they had gone
too far. It was not, however, their lumping together of ethical
and non-ethical evaluations under the heading of 'metaphysical' or 'meaningless' which troubled them. Apparently
their afterthoughts were solely confined to the fear that they
had been too cavalier in their attitude to Ethics. Mostly they
remained as far as ever from questioning the Moralist's claim
to ethical status for all value terms; although Carnap, who
later relented markedly from his former uncompromising attitude, actually came very near to the heart of the matter when
he wrote later:

> Moral value statements are meant by some philosophers as state-
> ments concerning the probable consequences of the acts in quest-
> ion. To call a kind of behaviour good or bad is meant as saying
> that it is a suitable or unsuitable way to a certain aim . . . On the

basis of any interpretation of this kind, e.g. in terms of intru-
mental function or of human interests or the like, a value
statement has obviously factual, cognitive content.[1]

How strange that Carnap should write of *moral* value statements when in the very act of conceding factual, cognitive
content to just those types of statement which are distinguished
by the fact that they are *not* derived from any moral imperatives
or any scheme of moral norms! Here by a hairsbreadth the
opportunity was missed of clearing up the moralistic muddle.
Schlick, by contrast, never came near it; though he devoted
an early work to the subject of Ethics, treating the Ought of
exhortation as a form of emotional appeal in the interests of
society, and value terms as the expression of hedonic 'drives'
and social pressures, and concluding with a plea for 'an Ethics
of Kindness' in contrast to the 'Ethics of Duty'.

4

Now this kind of thing is no answer to the Ethicist, who is still
entitled to ask, 'What of the Moral Sense, which may demand
action *running counter* to the interests of society? What of the
Law which makes a Higher claim than that of mere social
obligation?'
Such questions have to be dealt with somehow if we are
going to allow that there is *any* form of purely ethical statement
which can be significant. For if there is one kind of utterance
which is most surely entitled to be called ethical it is the kind
which demands action that *overrides* the claims of both personal
and collective expediency. But if, on the other hand, we are
going to find fault with the ethical statement or judgement on
the grounds that it is irrational, or on any other grounds, whilst
at the same time holding, with Carnap, that value statements
can be significant, our first step should surely be to draw a line
of demarcation between those value statements whose meaning
depends on some assumed 'absolute' or ultimate moral
authority, and value statements which claim to advance
testable propositions or state facts. There is no other way.
Repeated attempts have been made to formulate an ethic
which embraces all values under one head as 'ethical', but

[1] Footnote by Carnap in Lepley's *Verifiability of Value*, p. 138, n. 14.

all of them have foundered on one rock: the impossibility of reconciling actual desires, predilections, aims, and considerations of what is individually and collectively beneficial with the idea of a Higher authority which tells us to do *not* what we think will benefit us or satisfy our desires, but what is Right or our Duty. This is the aspect which must be isolated if we are to treat of Ethics in any comprehensive way, and not waste our time on what may turn out to be nothing but a futile attempt to rationalize the irrational, or an equally futile wrangle about words.

5

Religious believers mostly identify Duty with obedience to what is enjoined upon them by their God. The fact that we sometimes desire to do good, and that this desire may overcome our spontaneous impulses is even used by many Christian Ethicists as proof of the existence of a divine lawgiver. The assumption is that such desires are so contrary to human nature that only moral pressure from a supernatural source can possibly account for them.

According to some religious authorities the divine commands which it is our Duty to obey are all laid down in sacred writings such as the Bible: this was Locke's view. Others, notably Bishop Butler (who, however, firmly believed that benevolence is natural to man), held that Duty is made manifest in the promptings of Conscience, which directly transmits God's commands to the believer. Both schools, by insisting on a divine source for the idea of Duty were perhaps more logical in their approach than those who tried to derive it from human values, seeing that the very notion of Duty depends, one might think, on belief in a supreme Person to whom that duty is owed. The sense of Duty must, it would seem, derive from a sense, however vague, of an authority issuing commands. (Kant's Duty, however, carries its own authority, as it were, within itself.) The statement 'It is your Duty to do this' or 'You Ought to do this' is easier to understand and accept if the person who utters it can answer the question 'Who says so?' or 'Why is it my Duty?' It is a common criticism of agnostic Moralists that they have deprived themselves of all rational grounds for making any ethical pronouncements at all. Duty, say their critics, cannot be spontaneously generated; it must obviously have its origin in Someone who lays it down.

Still, there is no doubt that this Someone may be conceived in pretty impersonal terms. Evolutionary Ethicists, for example, write of Evolution simply as a 'process' and deny that they think of it as a kind of disembodied consciousness with a will of its own; yet at the same time they exhort us, in effect, though not in so many words, to do what It requires of us. Thus Julian Huxley tells us that 'Man's destiny is to be the agent of the evolutionary process.'[1]

This doctrine has interesting affinities to Aristotle's teaching about the Highest function of man, except for the necessarily more static nature of Aristotle's conception in an age when Evolution in the modern sense had not been thought of. We find in Evolutionary Ethics the very same suggestion that Man *as such* has a Duty to Something, which Duty is to consist in realizing his Highest potentialities. (But Aristotle was not burdened with the problem which must trouble evolutionary Ethicists no less than primitive Christians, of how to sustain the force of the ethical Ought whilst being committed to a belief in a scheme of things which is already beyond criticism or improvement.)

6

The position of moral philosophers who, though they do not believe that man's Duty is actually and literally laid down by a non-human authority, cling to the notion of ultimate Duty itself, is much less clearly defined. Some Ethicists find it necessary to presuppose a divine lawgiver so as to give meaning to their ethical maxims. In some of Kant's observations we seem to find him accepting Voltaire's dictum that if God did not exist it would be necessary to invent him; but elsewhere he writes like a believer, and derives proof for the objective existence of God from the alleged necessity that moral virtue should be posthumously rewarded. Yet a characteristic doctrine in the *Metaphysic of Morals* is that of Autonomy: 'The

[1] *Proceedings of the First International Congress on Humanism and Ethical Culture*, 1952, p. 18.

Laws to which man is subject are only those of his own giving.'[1]
Here Kant denies that we need an external moral legislator.

Sidgwick is an example of an Ethicist who belongs to the
Postulators rather than the Believers. He writes of a 'moral
order of the world' as an *assumption* 'which is normal to reflective
man'[2] but he never quite comes off the fence on either side.
Sidgwick was troubled by the desire to find a logical ethical
justification for a strong personal conviction of his that the
absolute and ultimate Duty of everybody is to do good to his
fellows. He wanted a stronger argument than a mere appeal
to intuition, and so, with a hint of reluctance, he adopted the
standpoint that the situation required a God who would
reward human goodness in the hereafter.

The Benthamite Utilitarians had no scruples about rejecting
the idea of God as a necessary basis for Ethics. They held that
to increase the sum of happiness was a self-evident paramount
Duty, and that the Right action on every occasion was to raise
the hedonic level or prevent it from sinking, as the case might
be. But because they equated good will and good activity with
moral Goodness the Utilitarians were all guilty of the self-
contradictions which are inseparable from Moralism. Inasmuch
as they wrote in the character of Ethicists, not merely giving
advice about means to happiness, but also using the language
of moral exhortation, they were compelled to juggle with value
terms, and this more especially because, not being Theists,
they could not make their 'ought' stand for an obligation to
any supreme authority, whilst at the same time, as Ethicists,
they had to make it look more authoritative than the 'ought'
of expediency (if you want ... then you ought to ...). The
resulting muddles and self-contradictions were the price they
had to pay for giving good advice dressed up as moral maxims,
and trying to equate ethical values with basic ones. Even
Bentham, who had very little to say about Duty, fell headlong
into the trap of Moralism, as will appear.

Not that the Utilitarians were more ambiguous in their use
of value terms than other Ethicists; very few in fact have ever
managed to avoid such ambiguity. And this brings us to the
question of whether there *can* be such a thing as a pure ethic.

---

[1] From *Kant's Theory of Ethics*. Abbott, p. 51.

[2] *The Ethics of Green, Spencer, and Martineau*, p. 188.

7

By a pure ethic I mean a general principle of Right or Moral conduct which (a) does not consist partly of advice, and (b) is innocent of Moralism.

With regard to (a): To advocate beneficence, or any other sort of conduct, on the ground that it will be advantageous on earth, or that it will pay dividends in the hereafter, is to issue advice. To say, 'If you want eternal bliss this is the way to get it' is no more to utter a moral exhortation or enunciate an ethical principle than it would be to say 'If you want a legacy you must make a fuss of your uncle'. Kant saw this, and his rewarding God was not meant to serve as an inducement, but was conceived firstly to account for the feeling of moral obligation or Duty, and secondly to satisfy what Kant regarded as the 'formal' requirement that there should be divine justice. In this respect, therefore, his ethic passes the test for purity, unlike Sidgwick's; for Sidgwick, with Butler and all orthodox Christian Ethicists other than the Predestination school, treats desire for the promised heavenly reward, and the fear of Hell, as sound practical reasons for behaving in the required way.

With regard to (b): No ethic which compromises with the 'ought' of mere expediency or the 'good' of mere beneficence can claim to be pure. To introduce Moralism into Ethics produced chaos by mixing up basic values with the Values of Ought, Right, and Duty.

8

The question whether there can be a pure ethic is not the same as the question whether a pure moral *act* is possible, but it is convenient to approach it by considering this latter question first, because it is the pure moral act which any pure moral principle, as well as any pure moral exhortation, must require of us. If we accept the consistent strict Ethicist's criterion for a moral act: that it must be an act of Duty or of obedience to a Higher authority than one's own desire, it follows that to be moral an act must not be done with an aim in view (*vide* the quotation from Kant at the head of this chapter). This condition means, at the very least, that the act must not be done for the sake of bringing about a particular desired result; but even so we might consider that an act done so as to conform to the general *principle* that we have chosen to embrace might fairly be called moral. However, the obvious difficulty about this view is that not every act that we do 'on principle' is entitled to be called moral, since besides what are called 'moral principles' there are principles of expediency: such principles, e.g. as those we embrace and follow for the sake of the community in whose advantages we are conscious that we share. In such cases we have a sort of generalized desire to follow our principle even though doing so may not always suit our convenience. Ultimately we try to follow it for our own purposes and not because we feel that to do so is Right. Further, our own purposes would be just as much the decisive thing if the principles were based on the wish to live up to a personal ideal: to be a better parent, say, or to be a braver, or a more popular, or impressive, person than we are at present. A man who disciplines himself in accordance with a principle may have many possible motives, from motives connected with money-making to more simple emotional ones such as the wish to be liked or feared, or simply to resemble some person that he admires.

So if a moral act is an act done 'on principle' the principle must be of some special kind. It must, in fact, be a moral principle, and this does not get us any nearer to finding our criterion.

9

However, the main objection to trying to define the moral act as an act done in accordance with a principle is that this would mean denying the title of moral to that very class of act which seems most certainly to deserve it. I mean the act which results from a *direct intuitive conviction* that it is Right, or the agent's Duty, to do it. There seems very little doubt that such a conviction is often experienced and sometimes acted upon, and it is here, surely, that we find morality in its simplest and purest form. If we recognize the feeling of moral con- viction—the immediate 'knowing' that to do *this* is Right, or is Wrong, as a distinct identifiable experience which can produce either spontaneous acts or, similarly, acts done in obedience to a conviction, felt at the time, that a Right principle demands them absolutely, I think we have arrived at what every morally-minded person regards as the primary condition for purely moral action. To say that an act can be moral even though its agent does *not* feel that it is Right to do it, or equally, to deny that some act is moral even though its agent *does* feel that it is Right to do it is virtually to rob morality of its most distinctive characteristic, and the one by which the moral agent himself identifies it.

Though it is not altogether surprising that many people, even highly moral people, refuse to accept the view that this intuitive moral certainty, or what Kant called 'the moral feeling', is the only source of true morality, their reasons as a rule are not respectable. They deny moral status to other people's intuitions because they want to regard their own as universally valid.

10

We seem, then, to have narrowed down the pure moral act to an act done *from* a special feeling, as distinct from any act done 'on purpose'. I call this distinctively moral feeling *the sense of Duty*, which is what it is probably most often called by those who find themselves actuated by it ('Conscience' seems sometimes to mean the same thing, but I avoid this word because conscience is a less pure concept than the sense of Duty; being often allowed—as by Bishop Butler—to be a feeling connected with ideas of what is expedient in the long run.)

A possible objection to calling it thus is that though the 'moral feeling' may be experienced as the obligation to obey a superior Being or at least a superior Will, it may equally well be an even more immediate experience; as immediate, say, as the 'being shocked' of a conventional person in the face of an impropriety. This seems to leave no room for a feeling of Duty *to* anything. Yet I think this objection loses most of its force if we accept what psychologists tell us about the origin in childhood of the Duty-feeling. For they trace it back to a source in the commands of parents: commands which were reinforced by threats and promises, or simply by demonstrations of pleasure and displeasure. These impressions are said to soak in with the passage of time and the consequent blurring of memories, till the awareness of an external authority becomes transformed into a sense of an internal authority: the undying echo of the parent's admonishing voice.

As Nietzsche put it: 'The content of our conscience is that which was, without any given reason, regularly *demanded* of us in our childhood by people we honoured or feared.'[1] In this way complicated feelings of love and fear become detached from their source and take on a kind of independent existence as a generalized feeling of obligation or Duty to behave in this way or that (though they may be transferred to other objects —gods or political parties). So if the psychologists are right, morality, in whatever direction it may develop, is deeply rooted in a disposition to submit one's will and judgement to a superior authority in uncritical obedience. (Though this interpretation would certainly not have been acceptable to Kant.)

It still remains possible to question, with Kant, whether a purely moral act has ever in fact been performed: an act, that is, which is done *only* from Duty without the least influence from any sort of positive or negative desire; but this is a psychological question which in the last resort can only be settled by the moral agent himself; and why, after all, should we go out of our way to question the impressions of those who sincerely believe that they do, sometimes, perform strictly moral acts? I should say that on the whole there is least reason to doubt that the pure sense of Duty was at work in cases where a strong instant conviction of Right or Wrong is felt, and rather more reason to doubt it when acts are done so as to conform to a general principle of conduct or a set of moral values which has been previously embraced. For a principle previously accepted without question as Right may suddenly lose its authority in face of a new moral conviction demanding action which runs contrary to it: the experience of Saul on the road to Damascus might be a case in point. And if in spite of the new conviction the principle were still adhered to, and allowed to override the new moral impulse, I think we should have

[1] From *The Wanderer and his Shadow*, quoted by R. Hollingdale, *Nietzsche*, 1965.

to say that the action so taken was at any rate *less* moral than action in response to the new prompting would have been.

II

Before raising the immediate question whether a 'pure' ethic can be formulated—whether, that is to say, it is possible for one pure Duty-principle or set of pure Duty-principles to be laid down for oneself or others to follow—it will be as well to touch first on the allied question of whether there can be any 'pure' ethical *utterances*, whether or not based on a system, directed to influencing conduct.

In Chapter 3 I examined the *Ethics* of Aristotle with a view to seeing if it contained any ingredient which could be called purely ethical. I concluded that it passed the test in that it carried implicit *exhortations* to live up to a Duty-ideal. An exhortation is not a statement, but is intended as a special sort of direct appeal to the hearer's 'feelings', and I think we may agree now that the particular 'feeling' which is meant to be affected by exhortations is this same sense of Duty that we have isolated. This might be expressed by saying that to produce their effect moral exhortations must touch, as it were, the sense of Duty and cause it to vibrate. This is only a very loose metaphor, and no doubt it is a crude way to represent a complicated experience which has many mysterious features. Whether an exhortation can really make a clean impact on the sense of Duty without at the same time touching certain desires—the desire to feel virtuous, for example, or to retain one's self-respect—is a doubtful matter; but if it is to *any* extent effective as a direct stimulus to the sense of Duty then it seems fair to say that it fulfils its intended function as a true moral exhortation, quite irrespective of what its content may be.

On this view the 'ethicalness' of an exhortation is to be judged neither by its form nor its content, but by its intended effects; so that an utterance might have the grammatical form of a factual statement and yet be a true moral exhortation, if it were meant to stimulate the Duty-sense. Thus, e.g. 'No honourable man would do such a thing!' might be just as much a moral exhortation as 'Be honourable!' The words could in theory be anything comprehensible so long as they conveyed no appeal to desire or liking; only, to be *effective* morally, they would have not to exhort the hearer to do anything which violated what his sense of Duty already accepted as Right.

12

We come at length to the main question: Is a pure ethic possible?

Now if we accept the moral agent's own view, as surely we must, that he acts morally when, and only when, he is obeying his sense of Duty, it follows that no general ethical principle can be laid down unless there is at least one type of action which every sense of Duty will always dictate. But this will be hard to find. None of the ordinary social virtues such as veracity and honesty are universally accepted as ultimately moral, since a God or a deified Process may always demand an ultimate loyalty which requires the believer to flout them. Conversely, a conviction like the one so passionately affirmed by A. Koestler that 'the end never justifies the means' might produce a fanatical adherence to conventional virtues which is just as moral. The moral experience is unique and private in each moral person, being the outcome of his individual history.

It is true that in a community closely bound by conventions a sort of collective moral sense may seem to prevail, but few people would deny that the sense of Duty may be just as pure in the rebel who breaks away as it is in those who continue to conform. Even the man who betrays his country's secrets to a foreign power may be actuated by his sense of Duty as much as is the man who chooses to die rather than reveal them. (On the other hand, of course, neither may be acting morally, but only from the conscious and deliberate aim of promoting some end he favours, or preventing something he has reasons for wanting to prevent.)

It seems necessary to conclude that almost any sort of action may be Right for somebody, and that there is hardly any sort of action that is Wrong for everybody.

To argue, as some people do, that this state of affairs yields at least one general moral principle, namely the Duty of being tolerant, its only a piece of moralistic special pleading. No general moral principle that tolerance is Right can be derived from the fact that *anything* may be Right. On the contrary, it means that intolerance can be just as Right as tolerance. To persecute and punish others for conduct which your own sense of Duty condemns is certainly moral if you happen to entertain that seemingly very common moral conviction that it is a Duty to coerce others into accepting—or at least submitting outwardly to—one's own moral principles.

What ethical values, then, are left to be stated in general terms? Clearly, none. For if Duty is a matter of personal intuition *there can be no universal language of ethical evaluation.* The language of *basic* evaluation is universal because it is derived from assumptions, continually reinforced by observation, about the basic tastes in experience of every human being. Given these assumptions we can make statements about conduct in terms of its goodness and badness as it affects people: affects them in any of the innumerable ways in which people's feelings and interests can be favourable or adversely affected by the conduct of other people. *These* value statements are theories testable by experience, or they are propositions which can be debated by the light of what experience has already taught us. No such tests, no such experience, are necessarily relevant to ethically-determined Goodness or Badness, Rightness or Wrongness.

13

Yet in spite of these considerations I think there remains one pure ethical *principle* which is derived from a generally acceptable criterion for all moral *action.* For if the sole necessary condition for the moral act is that it must be done in obedience to the sense of Duty, we can express this as the general moral principle, *It is your Duty to obey your sense of Duty.*

It might be objected that the above only amounts to a definition: that all it really says is, 'Your Duty' means 'obedience to your sense of Duty.' In a way this is true, though we should notice here that 'It is your Duty to obey your sense of Duty' could in some circumstances amount to more than a definition, seeing that it could function as a moral exhortation; that is, it could stimulate the hearer's sense of Duty, especially when that sense is in conflict with desire or distaste or with considerations of expediency; though of course in so doing it would only act on the level of an *ad hoc* utterance and could not be regarded as a principle. But in any case I see no reason to reject the formula because it is a tautology.

There is another possible objection, however: An ethical principle must be general. That is, it must not apply only to particular cases; and it might be argued that 'It is your Duty to obey your sense of Duty' can only mean something to those people, possibly a minority, who do possess a sense of Duty. However, the condition that the principle must be general does not mean that it must be able to influence *anybody*, or even that it must be comprehensible to *anybody*. Just as Aristotle in advocating the life of contemplation emphasized that he was necessarily speaking only to those whom he assumed to be capable of imagining this sort of life, so the Ethicist who lays down a Duty-principle speaks only to those who intuitively understand the concept of their Duty. Moreover, as Kant said, 'Ought implies can', and nobody *can* apply a principle if he doesn't understand it. Therefore neither the fact that our principle may not apply to some people, nor the fact that to some it may be incomprehensible, is any ground for rejecting it.

Only one other possible objection suggests itself, and it is not really a valid one. From the fact that nobody can accept as a principle 'It is your Duty to obey your sense of Duty' unless he already possesses a sense of Duty, it follows that *nobody can apply it who does not already accept it*. Therefore *as a principle* it can never have any effect (though, as we have noticed, it might be effective as an exhortation uttered *ad hoc*). As a principle it must be just as ineffective as, say, the principle 'In order to walk you must put one foot in front of the other' laid down for someone who already knows how to walk. But this does not make the principle self-contradictory or illogical.

I think this disposes of the last objection to accepting 'It is your Duty to obey your sense of Duty' as the one, and the only, ethical first principle which can constitute a *pure* ethical system, completely independent of all non-ethical values.

14

We have now isolated the pure ethical principle, but in the process of pinning it down the consequence has emerged that so-called 'moral principles' which are to exert any influence on action (otherwise than as a kind of immediate jolt to the sense of Duty) must be *impure*, because they must contain open or tacit inducements to conform to them. Such appeals are in fact always made by the authors of prescriptive systems, and they involve that double or equivocal use of terms like 'ought', 'right', 'wrong', and 'good' which characterizes Moralism.

In the three chapters which follow I will try to show something of the great variety of forms which Moralism may take, and its pervasive influence in ethical theory of every kind, as well as the logical embarrassments to which it gives rise.

First I show how Moralism corrupts the system of that great apostle of pure Ethics, Kant; and in the following chapter how, from the opposite direction, it enters into, and likewise corrupts, the doctrines of Bentham.

After Bentham, partly as a direct effect of his influence, and partly in reaction against it, moral philosophy took a new direction, and the analysis of open value language as a means to discovering the nature of ethical judgements became a major preoccupation. This development has been extremely favourable to Moralism, and to show this I shall discuss (in Chapter 7) a distinguished example from the verbal-analysis school.

5

THE ETHICAL VALUES OF KANT

> *A deed is Right or Wrong in general* (rectum aut minus rectum) *according as it is consistent or inconsistent with Duty* (factum licitum aut illicitum) *no matter what the content or the origin of the Duty may be.*
>
> KANT

SUMMARY: This chapter is devoted to an analysis of the main distinctive features of Kant's system of Ethics, with special emphasis on the epoch-making development both in moral philosophy and in axiology brought about by his rigorous distinction between morally Good or Right (i.e. Duty-inspired) action on the one hand, and benevolently-inspired or beneficent action on the other. Kant's use of 'good' in his phrase 'the good Will' is the classic example of the *ethical* use of the term which *divorces it from all connotatians of benevolence or beneficence.* Nevertheless Kant afterwards tried by various means to close the breach, and so lapsed into the inconsistencies and self-contradictions typical of Moralism.

I

Kant is recognized as the great Rigorist of ethical theory. Sternly he cast out from the temple of Ethics all commerce in objects of desire; the useful, the expedient, the socially advantageous. How striking it is then, that after writing the famous opening sentence of his *Fundamental Principles of the Metaphysic of Ethics*[1]—'Nothing can possibly be conceived in the world, or

---

[1] Unless otherwise stated the quotations which follow are from Abbott's standard translation, *Kant's Theory of Ethics* (Longmans). I have ventured to tamper with Abbott's text by using initial capitals, where he does not, for terms such as Will, Reason, and Value wherever they seem to figure as part of Kant's *strict* ethical, or *strict* 'moral' vocabulary. As all nouns in German have initial capitals Kant could not make any such distinction himself, but it seems reasonable to assume that he

even out of it, which can be called good without qualification, except a good will'—Kant should at once have gone on to justify this pronouncement in words which appeal quite frankly to values which his 'good', i.e. moral, will was bound to set aside. In fact the appeal is to normal accepted ideas of desirable and undesirable human characteristics, and to show this I will italicize the terms and phrases which support Kant's argument that a good will is a good or beneficent thing, and its absence bad:

> Intelligence, wit, judgement, and the other talents of the mind, however they may be named; or courage, resolution, per-severence, as qualities of temperament, are undoubtedly good and desirable in many respects; *but these gifts of Nature may also become extremely bad and mischievous* if the will which is to make use of them . . . is not good . . . Power, riches, honour, even health, and that general well-being and contentment with one's condition which is called happiness *may inspire pride and often presumption* if there is not a good will *to correct the influence of these on the mind*, and with this also to rectify the whole prin-ciple of acting, and adapt it to its end (p. 9).

A good will or character is here *recommended* on various grounds. It is a safeguard against the possible bad and mis-chievous effects of courage, resolution, and perseverance, and against the unpleasant and dangerous pride and presumption which may result from being powerful, wealthy, honoured, healthy, or happy.

So we see that in the opening paragraph of the *Fundamental Principles* 'good' is used in the *basic* sense: the sense which con-notes *benefit*, when Kant is referring to advantages such as the possession of the sort of gifts which enable a man to prosper in the world; and when he writes of a good *will*, which, he says, mitigates the possibly harmful effects of these 'good and desirable' gifts, a part of its goodness seems to consist in its performing this good office. Kant proceeds to elaborate the notion of the good will as follows:

---

would have done so, in some cases at least, if he had been writing in English. I have amended Abbott's use of the small 'n' for personified Nature; also, in cases where he translates Kant's 'Werth' as 'worth' I have for the sake of consistency amended it to 'value'. My quotations in German are from the *Akademie* edition of Kant's collected works, as are also my own translations from the German.

F

The good will is good not because of what it performs or effects, not by its aptness for the attainment of some proposed end, but simply by virtue of the volition, that is, it is good in itself, and considered by itself is to be esteemed much higher than all that can be brought about by it in favour of any inclination ... Even if it should happen that ... this will should wholly lack power to accomplish its purpose, if with its greatest efforts it should yet achieve nothing, and there should remain only the good will (not, to be sure, a mere wish, but the summoning of all means in our power) then like a jewel, it would still shine by its own light, as a thing which has its whole value in itself. Its usefulness or fruitfulness can neither add to nor take away anything from this value. It would be, as it were, only the setting to enable us to handle it the more conveniently ... or to attract to it the attention of those who are not yet connoisseurs, but not ... to determine its value (p. 10).

So far we might imagine that Kant is still standing on the same ground, and that he is calling attention in rather rhetorical language to two important facts about our attitude to good will. First, there is the fact that by 'good will' we mean good nature or good intentions, not good performance. Good intentions may come to nothing, and we might speak of a man as having a heart full of good will, without necessarily implying that he has been able to *do* any good at all, just as we may speak of 'good' food which in the event is wasted. To this extent it is quite true to say that good will is 'good in itself'; we call it good though its goodness may be a latent sort of goodness corresponding, say, to the latent 'powerfulness' of an engine which has never yet been put to use.

Secondly, there is the psychological fact that we tend to value benevolence as such very highly, and that we may think no less well of someone who has planned and worked to do something of great benefit to mankind because he was unlucky and failed.

But now in Kant's next sentence we find this:

There is, however, something so strange in this idea of the absolute value (*absoluten Werthe*) of will *per se* (*des blossen Willens*) in which no account is taken of its utility, that notwithstanding the thorough assent of even common reason to the idea, a suspicion must arise that it may perhaps really be the product of mere high-flown fancy, and we may have misunderstood the purpose of Nature in assigning reason as the governor of our will. Therefore we will examine this idea from this point of view.[1]

Reference has now been made to the *absolute* value of 'will *per se*', although nothing was previously said which necessarily implied that 'will *per se*' has 'absolute value'. All we were told was that a good will has supreme value irrespective of what it achieves, and this need not have meant more than that we, or at least the connoisseurs among us, place a good will highest in our scale of values: which assertion may be an exaggeration, but does not invoke any standard except that of human preference. But now these observations appear in a different light and we find that with the transformation of the supreme value of good will into 'absolute value of will *per se*', coupled with the highly significant reference to the purpose of Nature, the argument has moved decisively on to a higher plane.

2

The remarks which follow by way of introduction to Kant's theory of the Good (or Moral) Will are quite clearly intended to controvert Aristotle's doctrine that whereas Nature has decreed that man's excellence shall consist in the exercise of reason she has also decreed that he shall find his highest happiness thereby. Notice that this argument is quite explicitly made to depend on inferences about Nature's intentions in regard to man.

> In the physical constitution of an organized being, that is, a being adapted suitably to the purpose of life, we assume it as a fundamental principle that no organ for any purpose will be found but what is the fittest and best adapted for that purpose. Now in a being which has reason and a will, if the proper object of Nature were its *conservation*, its *welfare*, in a word, its *happiness*, then Nature would have hit upon a very bad arrangement in selecting the reason of the creature to carry out this purpose. For all the actions which the creature has to perform with a view to this purpose, and the whole rule of its conduct, would

[1] *Kant's Gesammelte Schriften.* Vol. IV, pp. 394-5.

be far more surely prescribed to it by instinct, and that end
would have been attained thereby much more certainly than
it ever can be by reason . . . Nature would not only have taken
on herself the choice of the ends, but also of the means, and
with wise foresight would have entrusted both to instinct.

And in fact, we find that the more a cultivated reason applies
itself with deliberate purpose to the enjoyment of life and
happiness, so much the more does the man fail of true satisfaction. And from this circumstance there arises in many, if they
are candid enough to confess it, a certain degree of *misology*,
that is, hatred of reason . . . and they end by envying, rather
than despising, the more common stamp of men who keep
closer to the guidance of mere instinct . . . And there lies at
the root of these judgements the idea that our existence has a
different and far nobler end, for which, and not for happiness,
reason is properly intended . . . (pp. 12–13).

This passage shows Kant accepting Aristotle's view that in
exercising his reason man is fulfilling Nature's Highest purpose
for him, and that the Highest type of man is the thinker; but
contradicting the other part of Aristotle's thesis, that the exercise of reason leads, and is meant to lead, to happiness.

It is worth noticing that the whole argument about Nature's
purpose in regard to man, which is supposed to demonstrate
that she did not endow him with reason as a means to his
happiness, depends upon Kant's identifying two concepts which
are usually thought of as entirely different, namely preservation
(*Erhaltung*) and happiness (*Gluckseligkeit*). Welfare (*Wohlergehen*)
is used as a kind of catalyst to unite the other two concepts thus,
'. . . its conservation, its welfare, in a word its happiness . . .'.
We are then told that if it had been Nature's real purpose to
secure our preservation-welfare-happiness she would not have
given us the faculty of reason to that end, but only instinct,
because instinct would have been more effective. The implication of this is that it was *not* Nature's real purpose . . . though
nothing has yet been said which actually supports this conclusion, even on Kant's own premises. All that has emerged
is two quite unsupported negative propositions, i.e. that
Nature's real purpose was not to secure man's preservation-
welfare-happiness, and that she did not endow him with reason
to that end. If we had been told only that Nature's purpose
cannot have been to secure our preservation, because if so she

would not have endowed us with reason, we should naturally have remarked that all the same, as it happens, we *have* so far been preserved, and anyhow, if Nature had not wanted us to survive why should she even have bothered to endow us with instincts? If on the other hand we had been told only that Nature's purpose cannot have been to secure our *happiness*, because if so she would not have endowed us with reason but only with instincts, we should have said that we do not see that this follows at all; and we might have added that actually our possession of reason seems if anything to point to the opposite conclusion about Nature's intentions, seeing that a creature which entirely lacked reason could hardly be capable of happiness. But through *identifying* happiness with preservation at the outset of the argument about the purpose of Nature, and then afterwards dropping the subject of preservation and concentrating on happiness only, Kant gives the confused reader the impression that some sort of proof or demonstration has really emerged to the effect that our reason cannot have been given to us for our happiness.

However, the purpose of the argument as distinct from its content is easy enough to grasp: it is an attempt to dispose of Aristotle's thesis about Nature's aims with regard to human reason and happiness so as to clear the ground for Kant's own doctrine that Nature's purpose in endowing us with reason was to produce in us a Will 'which is not merely good as a means to something else, but *good in itself*' (p. 12). Aristotle believed in a 'noble' function for man—the exercise of his reason in 'abstract meditation'—but he was not content to call the life of reason noble, he declared it to be delightful as well. This was quite unacceptable to Kant, partly because of his strongly puritanical disposition, but also because he saw that if reasoning is a means to happiness, even though it is not a form of sensual indulgence it may be engaged in *because* it is found to make for happiness; which meant that it could not serve as what Kant wanted it to be: an activity closely connected with Duty, or the moral Will. Therefore Kant set himself to convert reason to the service of Morality, and began by declaring that its 'true destination' must be to produce a Will which is 'good in itself'.

After this has been decreed, purely on the basis of a piece

of confused metaphysical speculation about the purpose of Nature, Kant goes on:

> We have, then, to develop the notion of a Will which deserves to be highly esteemed for itself, and is good without a view to anything further; a notion which exists already in the sound natural understanding, and requires rather to be clarified than to be taught, and which in estimating the value of our actions always takes the first place, and constitutes the condition of all the rest. In order to do this we will take the notion of Duty, which includes that of a Good Will, although implying certain subjective restrictions and hindrances. These, however, far from concealing it or rendering it unrecognizable, rather bring it out by contrast, and make it shine forth so much the brighter (p. 13).

The notion of 'deserving to be highly esteemed' is not elaborated any further here (later it comes up again as part of an account of the end of moral action). Mainly we are meant to concentrate on the concept of a Will being 'good without a view to anything further', i.e. being Good.

3

The following quotation exhibits the *purely ethical* side of Kant's doctrine, untinged by Moralism. The notion of Duty, we remember, 'includes that of a good Will', so that where the term Duty is used here we may take it to cover 'good Will' in Kant's sense, though labouring under 'certain subjective restrictions and hindrances'.

> ... it is always a matter of Duty that a dealer should not overcharge an inexperienced purchaser; and wherever there is much commerce the prudent tradesman does not overcharge ... but this is not enough to make us believe that the tradesman has so acted from Duty and from principles of honesty; his own advantage required it; it is out of the question in this case to suppose that he might besides have a direct inclination in favour of the buyers, so that, as it were, from love he should give no advantage to one over another. Accordingly the action was done neither from Duty nor from direct inclination, but merely with a selfish view.
>
> On the other hand, it is a Duty to maintain one's life; and, in addition, everyone has also a direct inclination to do so. But

on this account the often anxious care which most men take for it has no intrinsic value, and their maxim has no moral import. They preserve their life *as Duty requires*, no doubt, but not *because* Duty requires. On the other hand, if adversity and hopeless sorrow have completely taken away the relish for life, if the unfortunate one . . . preserves his life without loving it—not from inclination or fear, but from Duty—then his maxim has a moral value (pp. 13–14).

Leaving aside the two unsupported assertions that it is a matter of Duty that a dealer should not overcharge, and that it is a Duty to maintain one's life, the paragraph may be taken as illustrating what Kant wishes us to understand by Duty, moral value, intrinsic value, and Good Will, and as defining his conception of the nature of a true moral act. For here it is laid down in the clearest terms that the necessary condition for a moral act is that it must be performed *solely* in obedience to Duty or the Good Will.

A few passages chosen from the very many to the same effect will show the importance which Kant attaches to his condition that the Good or moral Will must not be a will which wants, or intends, or purposes anything, and that any act which is done for the sake of its intended result is not a moral act. This point is never never forgotten for long; it recurs again and again throughout all the four major ethical treatises.

It is clear . . . that the purposes which we may have in view in our actions, or their effects regarded as ends and springs of the will, cannot give to actions any unconditional or moral value. In what then can their value lie . . .? It cannot lie anywhere but in the *principle of the Will* without regard to the ends which can be attained by the action (p. 16).

The moral Law is . . . for the Will of every finite rational being a law of *Duty*, or moral constraint . . . No other subjective principle must be assumed as a motive, else whilst the action might chance to be such as the Law prescribes, yet as it does not proceed from Duty the intention . . . is not moral (p. 175).

An absolutely good Will, then, the principle of which must be a categorical Imperative, will be indeterminate as regards all objects, and will contain merely the *form of volition* generally . . . p. 63).

The moral Law is the sole determining principle of a pure Will
(p. 204).

[Ethics] cannot start from the ends which the man may propose
to himself and hence give directions as to the maxims he should
adopt. . . . Indeed if the maxims were to be adopted in accordance with these ends (which are all selfish) we could not properly speak of the notion of Duty at all (p. 293).

Kant applies his criterion with admirable consistency in distinguishing between the good or benevolent will and the Good
or moral will; that is between ethical and non-ethical goodness
in human motives:

To be beneficent when we can is a Duty; and besides this, there
are many minds so sympathetically constituted that, without
any other motive of vanity or self-interest, they find pleasure
in spreading joy around them, and can take delight in the satisfaction of others so far as it is their own work. But I maintain,
that in such a case an action of this kind, however proper,
however amiable it may be, has nevertheless no true moral
value, but is on a level with other inclinations, e.g. the inclination to honour, which, if it is happily directed to that which
is in fact of public utility and accordant with Duty, and consequently honourable, deserves praise and encouragement, but not
esteem. For the maxim lacks the moral import, namely, that such
actions be done *from* Duty, and not from inclination (p. 14).

An interesting point of comparison is also made here to bring
out the ethical superiority of Goodness over goodness:

Further still; if Nature has put little sympathy in the heart of
this or that man, if he, supposed to be an upright man,[1] is by
temperament cold and indifferent to the sufferings of others
. . . would not he still find in himself a source from whence to
give himself a far higher value than that of a good-natured
temperament could be? Unquestionably. It is just in this that
the moral value of the character is brought out, which is incom-
parably the highest of all, namely, that he is beneficent, not
from inclination, but from Duty (pp. 14–15).

Moreover,

This very feeling of compassion and tender sympathy, if it

[1] Thus Abbott; but Kant's parenthesis (*übrigens ein ehrlicher Mann*) would probably
be better translated as 'in all respects an upright man'.

preceeds the deliberation on the question of Duty and becomes a determining principle, is even annoying to right-thinking persons, brings their deliberate maxims into confusion, and makes them wish to be delivered from it and to be subject to law-giving Reason alone (p. 214).

The 'will' which wants to spread joy, or which is good-natured or compassionate is not a Good Will. Kant repeatedly emphasizes that the motive of doing good is never a moral motive. It is not merely that good (as distinct from Good) will may sometimes run counter to morality; it is that good will as a determining motive is incompatible with morality—because there must be no determining motive at all except the pure moral motive itself.

4

Having gazed with appropriate emotions on the icy peaks of Morality we must now return to the subject of Reason, and try to discover how the fact that Nature has endowed us with it as an alternative to instincts is connected with our possession of a Good or moral Will. And we very soon find that Reason, in one of its manifestations at least, has nothing whatever to do with what we call reasoning, any more than Will has to do with willing, or Good Will with good will. It has no connection at all with the consideration of practical problems, but is 'pure Reason' itself.

Here follow a few examples of Kant's use of the term 'Reason' in his development of his ethical theory:

... Reason of itself, independent of all experience, ordains what ought to take place (p. 24).

... *if Reason of itself alone* determines the conduct ... it must necessarily do so *a priori* (p. 44).

Further, the moral Law is given as a fact of pure Reason of which we are *a priori* conscious, and which is apodictically certain, though it be granted that in experience no example of its exact fulfilment can be found (p. 136).

Pure Reason of itself alone is practical, and gives (to man) a universal Law which we call the Moral Law (p. 120).

Sometimes Reason seems to be *identified with* the Good Will; sometimes it is what infallibly determines the latter. In any case, Reason, in this phase of the argument, as the pure ethical 'motive', seems indistinguishable in its functioning from that sense of Duty which we take to be operative when people perform those acts which they 'know' that they *have* to perform because to do so is Right.

It would be easy to conclude then that Reason—ordaining, *independently of all experience*, 'what ought to take place'—stands in Kant's system of Ethics simply for the prime mover to moral action, and *a fortiori* comes before any process of moral reasoning, even reasoning about principles to be adopted or rejected, seeing that it gives us the moral Law as 'a fact . . . of which we are *a priori* conscious'.

Now if one could really see the situation in this light the task of understanding the Kantian ethic would be reduced to a mere matter of translating a few of the terms he uses, taking 'Duty' as the key to the cryptogram. In this way we should translate both 'Will' and 'Reason' into 'Duty-impulse' or perhaps, 'Feeling of being compelled to obey the sense of Duty.' And the adjective 'good' as applied to 'Will' (Kant never writes, I think of 'good Reason') might be taken simply as equivalent to 'dutiful', employed as added emphasis to distinguish the 'Duty-Will' from the normal one. (It is true that this interpretation would mean discounting Kant's moralistic 'lead-in' which I quoted at the beginning of the present chapter; but perhaps we could treat this merely as a device for luring the amoral reader into the web of pure Ethics.)

This would leave us with an account of the purely ethical motive identical with the one which emerged from our analysis of Chapter 4 above, which yielded the principle 'It is your Duty to obey your sense of Duty': a principle which Kant himself states in his *Preface to the Metaphysical Elements of Ethics* as the 'general ethical command, "Act dutifully from a sense of Duty".' Here also he says:

> The greatest moral perfection of man is to do his Duty, and that *from Duty* (p. 303).

This principle, to which Kant himself, strangely enough, never gives a name, I shall from now on call 'The Law of Pure Duty'.

5

It would be a great comfort if we could really see Kant's
ethical teaching as nothing more nor less than an elaborate
exposition of the Law of Pure Duty; but, as anyone who has ever
heard of Kantian Ethics well knows, such a compact and simple
interpretation of the central doctrine would be a weak travesty
of the real thing, if only because it does not include that famous
character in the Kantian ethical cast, the majestic Categorical
Imperative.

Some time before he introduces the Categorical Imperative
Kant re-defines Duty as '*The necessity of acting from respect for
the Law*' (p. 16). ('Law' does not mean, of course, the law of
the land, but the Moral Law. 'Respect' is defined in a footnote
as 'The immediate determination of the Will by the Law and
the consciousness of this'.) Having thus impressed upon us the
compulsive nature of Duty Kant proceeds:

> But what sort of Law can that be, the conception of which
> must determine the will even without paying any regard to the
> effect expected from it, in order that the will may be called
> Good absolutely and without qualification? As I have de-
> prived the will of every impulse which could arise to it from
> obedience to any law, there remains nothing but the universal
> conformity of its actions to Law in general, which alone is to
> serve the Will as a principle, i.e. I am never to act otherwise
> than so *that I could also will that my maxim should become a universal
> law*. Here now, it is the simple conformity to law in general,[1]
> without assuming any particular law applicable to certain
> actions, that serves the will as its principle, and must so serve,
> it, if Duty is not to be a vain delusion and a chimerical notion
> (pp. 17–18).

Subsequently the Categorical Imperative is formulated as
'*Act only on that maxim whereby thou canst at the same time will that
it should become a universal law*', but before this point is reached
the line of the argument has shifted somewhat, so that it will
be best to trace its progress from the beginning.

To the purely negative condition for a moral act that it must
have no aim, the further condition seems now to have been

[1] *die blosse Gesetzmässigkeit überhaupt*, K.G.S. Volume IV, p. 402.

added that it must be the immediate outcome of an attitude called 'respect for the law'.

Now as a description of the moral feeling or sense of Duty 'respect for the Law' seems very near the mark, if we regard this Law as some sort of privately sensed 'supreme command'. Kant himself refers to 'the moral feeling' and describes it as 'the *subjective* effect that the Law exercises on the will' (p. 80). Elsewhere it is 'a susceptibility of the free elective will for being moved by pure practical Reason and its Laws' (p. 311).

But why, we naturally ask, should it be only a *universal* law which may command this particular kind of respect? Surely it is a psychological fact that this primary feeling of 'respect for the Law' may 'determine the will' to obey a god; and not even necessarily a universal god, but a tribal one. And even mere social taboos and conventions seem often to call forth the very same kind of spontaneous reverence. This interpretation of the passage therefore seems unsatisfactory, and we look for another.

Does Kant mean, perhaps, not that 'universal laws' are in fact the only ones which command primary respect, but that they *ought* to be the only ones which do? Unfortunately this would mean that Kant is legislating for the moral Will, which would violate his famous Principle of Autonomy, according to which the individual moral Will must always determine for itself what action is Right for its owner.

A third possible interpretation would have the advantage of being perfectly consistent with the principle that the moral Will must have no aim—i.e. the Law of Pure Duty. (To begin with I only try to interpret the *introductory* passage quoted above, and not the actual formulated Categorical Imperative itself, which in fact comes some way farther on in the same Section of the Fundamental Principles.)

In the first place—see the quotation—Kant notes that he has deprived the moral Will of everything which can determine it to act, except one thing which he expresses as 'the universal conformity of its actions to law in general, which alone is to serve the Will as a principle'. Now 'Law in general' could here be taken to mean *any* sort of felt or intuited authority which evokes the moral feeling, and indeed by the context it seems impossible that it should mean anything else. This law then, that 'Law in general' must be obeyed, is the Law of morality itself. In other words it is the Law of Pure Duty, which by its form is a *universal* law, applying to all moral wills. Thus the test for morality is to see whether the maxim according to which one proposes to act (a maxim is defined as 'the subjective principle of volition') is the law of Pure Duty, and this is found by deciding whether it could be willed to become a universal law. If not, then clearly it cannot be the Law of Pure Duty.

There remains, of course, the objection that other maxims besides the Law of Pure Duty can be willed to become universal laws, but at any rate it is a test, if only a limited one, and the point is driven home by the concluding reiteration that 'simple conformity to Law in general' is the condition for Duty. This interpretation also finds a kind of support in the Categorical Imperative itself as it is afterwards formulated, in the shape of two words which some translators[1] find so puzzling that they omit them, but which I believe to be highly significant. These are the words *'durch die'* which Abbott correctly translates as 'whereby': *'Act only on that maxim whereby thou canst at the same time will that it should become a universal law'*. How can a maxim enable *itself* to be willed to become a universal law? Logically, of course, it cannot. Yet if the maxim is regarded as the direct outcome of a feeling (of reverence) then it can in a sense *consist of* the (universal) law that that feeling should be attended to and should determine the actions of the person entertaining it.

6

So far, then, it might be just possible to believe that the Law of Pure Duty is still pure; but before the Categorical Imperative comes to be stated the argument has developed along paths which, to say the least, take it into very dubious company, whilst at the same time the concepts of universality and of willability both begin to lead double lives. For now, after discovering a truly distinctive and exclusive criterion for moral action no matter what form the action may take, Kant does

---

[1] e.g. J. Watson: 'Act in conformity with that maxim, and that maxim only which you can at the same time will to be a universal law.' *Selections from Kant* (p. 241).

violence to his own achievement by trying to derive from this very criterion a set of principles according to which some forms of action are moral and some are not! And it transpires at once that the term 'universal Law' stands not only for the original Law of Pure Duty but also for any one of a variety of possible principles of social behaviour, the *only* condition for which is that they must be such that they *can* be willed to be obligatory for everybody. What this does, and does not, involve, will presently appear.

To assist at the metamorphosis of the original moral Law, *Reason* is now brought back into the argument, but in the process its purity, too, becomes sadly impaired. In fact we are now to witness the shocking spectacle of a kind of Rake's Progress of Reason, from that which 'of itself, and independent of all experience, ordains what ought to take place' (p. 24), to that which enables us to think logically, and finally to that which shows us on which side our bread is buttered.

7

Kant's first illustration of a moral principle shows Reason no longer *a priori*, but, to start with, still free from any taint of expediency. It is 'the common reason of men in practical (i.e. morally practical) judgements'.

The moral aspirant asks this Reason, 'May I when in distress make a promise with the intention not to keep it?' The answer of Reason is No, because 'I can by no means will that lying should be a universal law. For with such a law there would be no promises at all . . .' (p. 19).

This as it stands can be taken as a *logical* answer of Reason. You cannot 'will' a *universal* law of lying or promise-breaking, because the very notion of promise-breaking derives from that of promise-keeping, and the very notion of lying derives from that of veracity. Similarly you cannot will as a universal law that all men should be servants, or that all men should be masters, because servant implies master, and vice versa. These 'moral laws' are unwillable, not because nobody in his senses could wish them to prevail, but simply because they are logically impossible concepts.

The distinction between what, on the one hand, is such

that no normal person could possibly desire it, and what, on the other hand, cannot be willed because it is logically absurd is easy enough to grasp, and surely the very last person one would expect to find confusing them is Kant himself. Yet the sentence beginning 'For with such a law there would be no promises at all . . .' goes on, '. . . since it would be vain to assert my intention . . . to those who would not believe my assertion, or who if they did so too hastily would pay me back in my own coin'. Here Reason is being practical with a vengeance. Indeed this remark seems such an astonishing irrelevance that one may at first suspect that it is a mere slip, especially since it is followed by the sentence, 'Hence my maxim, as soon as it should be made a universal law, would necessarily destroy itself'; which seems clearly to refer to the *logical* point which Reason made; and even more especially since this in turn is followed by another reference to the moral necessity of discounting all considerations 'of advantage accruing . . . to myself and even to others' (p. 19).

Yet it is a fact that after this point considerations of expediency, though freely interspersed with reminders that absolute disinterestedness is the hallmark of the moral act, are advanced to support a series of Duties which Kant instances as typical of those demanded by the original Categorical Imperative.

One such Duty, for example, is not to neglect one's 'natural gifts'. Some people do let their talents rust, Kant observes, but, 'a man cannot possibly *will* that this should be a universal law of Nature, or be implanted in us as such by a natural instinct. For as a rational being he necessarily wills that his faculties be developed, since they serve him, and have been given him, for all sorts of possible purposes' (p. 41). This cannot be intended as an argument of logic, and there is no suggestion, even, that the neglect by everybody to develop his faculties is an absurd conception. By way of reasons why a person cannot possibly will it we are told, firstly that a man *necessarily* wills that his faculties should develop—a piece of mere psychological dogmatism—and secondly that they have been given him and serve him for all sorts of possible purposes; an argument which seems to combine expediency with conventional piety in equal proportions.

Again, we are given the example of a man who is prosperous and who decides not to help others in distress. Kant argues that though he can choose to be thus callous and unhelpful he cannot will a universal law of callousness and unhelpfulness: 'For a will which resolved this would contradict itself inasmuch as many cases might occur in which one would have need of the love and sympathy of others . . .' (p. 41). Here 'willing' is simply desiring, and can hardly be anything else. We cannot *desire* a universal law whereby when we are in distress nobody would come to our aid. By the same token we cannot desire a universal law of any kind which we consider might involve inconvenience to ourselves.

After giving this example Kant appears to notice that something is amiss with his argument, and in an attempt to mend matters he hastily distinguishes between two *types* of Duty as revealed by his examples, thus:

> Some actions are of such a character that their maxim cannot without contradiction be even *conceived* as a universal law of Nature, far from it being possible that we should *will* that it *should* be so. In others this intrinsic impossibility is not found, but still it is impossible to *will* that their maxim should be raised to the universality of a law of Nature, since such a will would contradict itself. It is easily seen that the former violate strict or rigorous (inflexible) Duty; the latter only laxer (meritorious) duty. Thus it has been completely shown by these examples how all Duties depend as regards the nature of the obligation (not the object of the action) on the same principle (p. 42).

But 'laxer (meritorious) duty' is a kind of duty which derives from the idea of what one cannot *desire* to be a universal law, and the will which cannot 'contradict itself' by wishing a law to be universal which its owner would not *desire* to be universal is not a moral Will at all, according to the conditions Kant has himself laid down, but a will which has regard to its owner's *interests* in a general way. It is a *prudent* will, in contradistinction to a moral or Good one, which is 'Good without a view to anything further' (*vide* p. 13).

Henceforth, though the above-mentioned distinction between two types of Duty drops out of the discussion, and further emphasis is repeatedly laid on the moral necessity of complete disinterestedness, arguments of prudence are still freely resorted to. One famous instance is the article on *The supposed Right to tell Lies from benevolent Motives,* which was published twelve years after the *Fundamental Principles.*

Kant had proved that nobody could logically will lying to be a universal law; but he apparently believed, or at any rate hoped, that he had also proved the positive proposition that veracity *must* be morally willed by everyone to be a universal law. Therefore he was concerned to defend the view that to speak the truth is a Duty in all circumstances; and this he did as follows:

> Truth in utterances that cannot be avoided is the formal Duty of a man to everyone, however great the disadvantages that may arise from it to him or any other; and although by making a false statement I do no wrong to him who unjustly compels me to speak, yet I do wrong to men in general in the most essential point of Duty .... that is .... I cause that declarations in general find no credit ... For instance, if you have by a lie hindered a man who is even now planning a murder, you are legally responsible for the consequences. But if you have strictly adhered to the truth public justice can find no fault with you, be the unforeseen consequence what it may. It is possible that whilst you have honestly answered Yes to the murderer's question, whether his intended victim is in the house, the latter may have gone out unobserved, and so not have come in the way of the murderer, and the deed therefore not have been done; whereas if you had lied and said he was not in the house, and he had really gone out (though unknown to you), so that the murderer met him as he went and executed his purpose on him, then you might with justice be accused as the cause of his death. ... Whoever then tells a lie, however good his intentions may be, must answer for the consequences of it even before the civil tribunal, and must pay the penalty for them, however unforeseen they may have been; because truthfulness is a Duty that must be regarded as the basis of all duties founded on contract, the laws of which would be rendered uncertain and useless if even the least exception to them were admitted (pp. 362–3).

The argument throughout is one of expediency—the expediency of acting according to the principle of veracity—and one consideration put forward is that the person who conforms to the principle cannot be held legally responsible even if the

G

murderer kills his victim, whereas if he had lied and things went wrong he might be blamed.

Kant's reason for arguing like this was not of course that he wished to recommend the policy of keeping out of trouble no matter what the consequences to others might be. His purpose was to demonstrate by hook or crook the universal validity of his principle, and the only arguments he could find to serve him were, firstly, a consideration of social expediency—duties *founded on contract* are not derived from pure Duty but are social obligations either legally established or voluntarily agreed to on account of their practical advantages, to which Kant draws attention—and secondly, a consideration of personal expediency, viz. what would be the safest course for a person placed in the position of having to choose between adhering to the principle and disobeying it for humane reasons. It is worth noticing that sooner than relax his rule Kant was prepared to discount the remorse which the dedicated truth-speaker might feel if his truthfulness resulted in the fugitive's murder. Perhaps the sense of 'worthiness to be happy' would have been adequate compensation. Or perhaps as a truly moral man he would have felt no remorse, for humane feelings, we remember, are no part of morality. Anyhow, this example shows at least that despite his many reiterations that the only Law 'that we can reverence', i.e. the only truly moral law, must be pure, in the sense of being unrelated to any part of our system of desires, Kant readily resorted to considerations of personal, as well as social, benefit and harm when he felt himself confronted with the question, Why should I obey this maxim? even as in his advocacy of obedience to Duty in general he invoked the inducement of a feeling called 'Consciousness of Moral Worth', which sounds much more exalted than 'smugness', but which seems to come to much the same.

All these arguments from expediency, representing as they do a disorderly retreat from the farthest point ever before reached in the analysis of morality, have been a source of endless controversy among succeeding generations of Ethicists, and more especially because Kant himself never once admitted that any retreat had taken place at all. The ultimate and absolute distinction between the 'imperative' of expediency, called the 'hypothetical imperative', and the pure moral

Categorical Imperative is still reiterated over and over again, although it becomes apparent that even in the terms of the Categorical Imperative itself, in the stipulation that the maxim must be able to be *willed* to be a universal Law, Kant was actually admitting into the heart of his system the one concept which he had seemed above all determined to keep out of it: namely willing in the *ordinary* sense, as desiring; and, moreover, desiring for reasons: reasons in the *ordinary* sense, as rationally motivated grounds for adopting a principle of action.

It might be pleaded, of course, that Kant had no alternative; that he had to fall back upon reasons of expediency because no other sort of reason was to be found. He had to *advise* us to adopt his principles, or we should have had no reason to adopt them. This in a way is true; but it would still have been open to Kant to concentrate on the purely formal aspects, and admit, as he came near to admitting once or twice, their complete uselessness as a guide for conduct. He could have said that he did not intend them as guidance, but that on the contrary his aim was precisely to demonstrate that since morality demands the total subjugation of all motives it is unreasonable to expect that anybody should ever perform a voluntary moral act: that moral acts are *involuntary* and compulsive, like sneezing, or at best like scratching oneself—an impulse that it is possible to control. In this case, of course, he might have been asked to explain what is the good of moral imperatives, but he would have been free to answer quite consistantly that they are no good at all; they are only Good.

8

Most Kantian moralists, while they notice and deplore certain ambiguities and inconsistencies in Kant's moral doctrines claim that the criterion of universal willability for any principle or maxim is particularly valuable and important. They admire it on the grounds that it provides a sort of logical justification for principles of conduct which are socially desirable, or at any rate eminently fair and reasonable. They hold that given only the basic arbitrary condition—whether derived from assumptions about the purpose of Nature or the nature of man—that the moral Will or Reason can only respect universal laws, the

Categorical Imperative provides a universally practicable
system of rules whereby the moral act is always in conformity
with behaviour of the sort which we recognize as good.[1]

There are many indications that Kant himself thought this,
although he usually treated this consequence as a kind of lucky
accident; something which just happened to result from his
strictly logical approach to pure ethical theory.

I do not think it did result from his approach to pure ethical
theory, nor that the Categorical Imperative, however it may
be understood, is of much practical value as a guide to conduct.
For unless we read between the lines certain limiting conditions
which are never stated, and which would have played havoc
with the whole structure of the system if they had been stated,
the Categorical Imperative affords moral justification for both
fairness and unfairness, both beneficent conduct and harmful
conduct with complete impartiality. Further, I think that the
attempt to apply it would in many cases land one in insoluble
dilemmas. I will explain briefly why I do not find it possible to
accept the view that the Categorical Imperative is either very
beneficent in its tendency or very useful as a working principle.

It is admittedly true that certain 'universal laws', such as a
universal law of lying cannot, for logical reasons, be willed; so
that, according to the principle, if I am in a situation in which
I can either lie or tell the truth it is immoral to lie and moral
to tell the truth—provided, of course, that I do not tell it
because I *want*, or *prefer*, for any reason, to tell it (precluded by
the Law of Pure Duty). But a law of lying is one among only
a very small group of self-contradictory 'universal laws' of

[1] Professor Paton argues that the purpose of Kant's insistence that moral laws
must be universal was to ensure that no moral Will should dictate conduct which
necessitated the coercion of another moral Will:

> Since Kant's universal laws are laws of freedom, this means that in determining
> my actions I have to take into account the rational Wills of other men: I ought
> to act in such a way that as rational beings they can act on the same law as I.
> Hence their rational Wills limit my actions . . . (*The Good Will*, p. 178).

But the 'Principle of Autonomy' is a law of freedom for the individual moral
Will; not a 'law of freedom' in the sense of freedom from coercion by outside
agencies—even other moral Wills. The condition of universality is actually incompatible with the Principle of Autonomy. For to lay down the condition that the
Law must be of a certain kind, namely a universal law, is to legislate for the
individual moral Will and impose limiting conditions. Kant himself says almost
nothing to substantiate Paton's interpretation. (But see the quotation given by
Russell, cited in section 11 below.)

conduct; laws which can, in a way, be thought of, but which are then seen at once to be absurd. The closely related 'universal laws' of lying, cheating, and promise-breaking seem pretty well to exhaust the list. And in fact the principles of not breaking promises and not lying or cheating are the only self-supporting universally willable principles which Kant himself derives from the Categorical Imperative: the considerations of expediency with which he tries afterwards to recommend them are gratuitous. But the other principles mentioned—not to waste natural gifts and not to behave callously—he felt obliged to shore up in this way, because obviously it would really be quite *logical* to will that all human beings should waste their talents, or to will that everyone shall subscribe to the maxim 'Each for himself and the Devil take the hindmost'.

In a sense it is true that to will a universal law of *injustice* would be as impossible as to will a universal law of lying, because there must be justice for there to be injustice; but justice and injustice are actually such vague and elastic concepts that a universal law which most people would certainly call unjust could quite well, logically, be willed: such a law, for example, as that the strong shall always be allowed to impose their wishes on the less strong. (That the less strong would not be very likely to welcome this universal law is, of course, beside the point, because the question only relates to what we are not debarred by *logic* from willing: it has nothing to do with whether you or I or anyone else would be at all likely to will it.)

One can think of plenty of *logically* willable universal laws of conduct which demand behaviour of the most ruthless and Nietzschean kind. Thus the Categorical Imperative in its pure unadulterated form is no barrier to conduct which is in basic terms strictly *bad*. This is not a logical objection, of course; illogicality only enters with the ill-judged attempt, of which Kant himself was guilty, to show that morality pays; or to squeeze some drops of the milk of human kindness out of the cold hard stone of the Good, or Moral, Will. As to the practical value of the idea of universally willable laws: even if we assume that by some lucky dispensation of Nature the only principles or maxims that anybody ever does will to be universal laws are in fact just those Duties which Kant specifies—e.g. 'It is a Duty to maintain one's life' (p. 19) and 'To be beneficent when one can is a Duty' (p. 14), the Categorical Imperative cannot give us any guidance on how to behave when it is necessary to violate one Duty so as to perform another. Thus I do not think the Categorical Imperative can be of much value in a general way, not of much help in particular situations. It is no obstacle to the most arbitrary and unjust principles—such for example as may originate in religious conviction and be derived from the maxim 'Everybody Ought to conform to the doctrines of the Catholic (or Lutheran, etc., etc.) Church.'

From the purely ethical standpoint none of the above matters in the least. The defects of the system are due to the fact that Kant *himself* was not reconciled to the sterility of his Moral Law, the Law of Pure Duty. Not that he ever doubted its transcendent sublimity, however. His chief concern was still to imbue others with his reverence for the idea of pure morality, and devotion to the ideal of self-discipline; a personal idiosyncrasy whose counterpart was contempt, frequently expressed, for ordinary tastes and pleasures. Moral *Value* is a constantly recurring theme; a value in no way associated with normal human values, but one deriving from a transcendent ideal which was to be approached through the suppression of all our natural impulses, including, quite logically, those which produce acts of spontaneous kindness.

Thus it was in no humanely relenting spirit that Kant allowed considerations of expediency to be peeped at through the fingers of pure moral reverence. From first to last, in spite of the self-interested calculations which are allowed to insinuate themselves into the moral argument, Kant never once lets kindness trespass on the Moral field. God or Nature might harbour benevolent designs for man; man himself has a Duty to be, when possible, beneficent, but good nature is no part of morality, and is indeed almost to be deplored, as a hindrance to Duty and the Good Will (see the quotation in section 3 above). In this one regard at least Kant is perfectly consistent. To be moral an act must be performed *on principle*. To begin with, the Moral Will is allowed to operate only on the principle of conformity to the Law of Pure Duty. Later, less pure principles are admitted (even a principle of expediency, it would seem, is Better than no principle at all). But still spontaneous 'inclination' is consistently excluded, and no action taken *for the sake of* the good of other people, whether individually or collectively, can be moral. Yet though the Kantian ethic is exceptional in its banning of benevolence as a moral motive, Kant has been justly praised as a champion of human dignity and of freedom for the individual, on account of his famous maxim '*So act as to treat humanity, whether in thine own person or in that of any other, in every case as an end withal, never as means only* (p. 47).

Those who are distressed by Kant's moral austerities cite this Imperative as evidence of a humane and even liberal bias in its author; and there is indeed a great deal of evidence for this in Kant's other writings. But the point to be noticed here is that this Imperative is *not* based on the original Categorical Imperative, let alone the Law of Pure Duty, and that it has no logical connection with either. Instead it is directly linked to the transcendent, intuitive, concept of 'absolute (moral) value' which we are to accept without question as sublime.

The new Imperative is introduced via a distinction between 'subjective' or 'relative' ends—i.e. ends which are the outcome of desires—and 'objective ends' which 'depend on motives valid for any rational being'. (Motives here are not of course motives in the normal sense, but 'moral laws' in operation.) Kant continues:

> Supposing, however, that there were something *whose existence* has *in itself* an absolute value, something which, being *an end in itself*, could be a source of definite laws, then in this and this alone would lie the source of a possible categorical Imperative, i.e., a practical law.
>
> Now I say: man, and generally any rational being, exists as an end in himself, *not merely as a means* to be arbitrarily used by this or that will, but in all his actions, whether they concern himself or other rational beings, must always be regarded at the same time as an end (p. 46).

So we see very clearly that the Imperative which demands that people should not be used as mere means to ends is not derived from, but is rather set up to justify, the Moral Law and the Categorical Imperative.

Kant goes on to repeat some previous remarks about the merely 'conditioned' value of objects of desire, which objects he now contrasts with persons, 'whose very nature shows them to be ends in themselves', and he adds that if this were not so 'nothing whatever would have absolute value'; and that 'if all value were conditioned and therefore contingent, then there would be no supreme practical principles of Reason whatever' (p. 46). The meaning of this seems to be that there must be something which has 'absolute value' or there could be no morality, so man himself must have absolute value because it is he who entertains this concept.

That persons are ends in themselves is repeated many times, now in support of the view that they must not be used merely as means, now as justification for the moral Law. Kant also contends that a man is only really free when controlling his impulses, because then only is his will not determined by anything external to it. This is an illuminating idea, but the argument that this self-determining Will, *because* it is self-determining, can only will actions which conform to maxims which can be willed to become universal laws is not a success:

> Physical necessity is a heteronomy of the efficient causes, for every effect is possible only according to this law, that something else determines the efficient cause to exert its causality. What else then can freedom of the will be but autonomy, that is the property of the will to be a law to itself? But the proposition: The will is in every action a law to itself, only expresses the principle, to act on no other maxim than that which can also have as an object itself as a universal law. Now this is precisely the formula of the Categorical Imperative and is the principle of morality, so that a free will and a will subject to moral laws are one and the same (pp. 65–66).

This is the best Kant can do by way of deriving the Moral Law from the concept of free will.

As to the implication that self-control is the same thing as morality: We all know that self-control may be practised for any number of reasons, none of which are at all moral in the strict Kantian sense; as by the sweet-loving person who eschews cream buns for fear of getting fat; by the sociable student who shuts himself up alone to work for an examination; by anybody who acts on the principle 'Look before you leap'.

Kant appears to equate the characteristic of being a person, a rational being, and an end in oneself with the ability to pursue pure moral ends; but the only reason we are given as to why there should be such literally aimless ends is—because the notion of a moral Law requires it:

> For since there are free actions, there must be also ends to which as an object those actions are directed. Amongst these ends there must also be some which are at the same time (that is, by their very notion) Duties. For if there were none such, then since no actions can be without an end, all ends which practical reason might have would be valid only as means to other ends, and a *categorical* Imperative would be impossible; a supposition which destroys all moral philosophy (p. 295).

And one which for this reason, if for no other, must not be entertained for a moment.

Kant himself seems to be aware that his new subsidiary Imperative has turned out after all to be but a shaky prop for the moral law, and in the passage I am going to quote, Nature's designs once more do duty as an ultimate source of Duty.

> Looking back now on all previous attempts to discover the principle of morality, we need not wonder why they all failed. It was seen that man was bound to law by Duty, but it was not observed that the laws to which he is subject are *only those of his own giving*, though at the same time they are *universal*, and that he is only bound to act in conformity with his own Will; a Will, however, which is designed by Nature to give universal laws (p. 51).

(This argument recalls the doctrine developed in the *Critique of Pure Reason* that it is man himself who is the author of what he calls natural laws—the laws which appear to us to govern events in the physical world; but what this really has to do with a self-regulating moral Will is by no means clear.)

I do not think anybody can explain just what is involved in the above statement that a man is 'bound to act in conformity with his own Will'. And even if we could somehow manage to endow it with a meaning, nothing, surely, could follow from it as to how men Ought to treat one another.

The assertion that a man is *bound* by universal laws to Duty really suggests that these laws are external to the personal moral Will and control it. This objection Kant tries to meet by reiterating his statement that the Will regards itself as giving laws:

Thus the Will is not subject simply to the Law, but so subject that it must be regarded *as itself giving the law* (of which it can regard itself as the author) (p. 49).

But this is found to be inadequate after all, because it does not follow that the laws are necessarily moral or that they have any special claim to be obeyed. The fact that the person who lays them down for himself probably wants or intends, for sound practical reasons, to obey them, far from being a recommendation, in Kant's moral terms, imperils their claim to be moral at all. Thus it is necessary to endow them, under Nature, with some extra authority, and so it is again asserted that they are universal laws, which again raises the difficulty about personal self-determination, and so on. These arguments are repeated over and over again with slight variations and with further invocations of Reason; but all in vain, and finally with an effect of exhaustion Kant admits that he cannot explain how a Categorical Imperative is possible:

> The question then: How a categorical Imperative is possible can be answered to this extent that we can assign the only hypothesis on which it is possible, namely, the idea of freedom; and this is sufficient for the *practical exercise* of reason, that is, for the conviction of the *validity of this Imperative*, and hence of the moral law; but how this hypothesis itself is possible can never be discerned by any human reason (p. 81).

But in fact the question how the hypothesis of freedom is possible is not in any way specially related to the idea of the Categorical Imperative or the Moral Will. In so far as there is a problem it applies equally to all voluntary—as distinct from *in*voluntary—acts; to all acts of the sort that we regard ourselves as choosing to perform in preference to others that we could have performed instead.

10

There remains the teaching that a man has value and dignity and that he must be let alone to work out his own salvation. This seems undoubtedly a good principle even though the value and dignity are accorded to man solely on the ground that he has a 'moral nature', or in other words, a capacity for self-control. The other side of human nature, with all its desires and tastes, inclinations and affections, is contemptible:

> All the inclinations together (which can be reduced to a tolerable system, in which case their satisfaction is called happiness) constitute *self-regard* (solipsismus). This is either the *self-love* that consists in an excessive *fondness* for oneself (philautia), or satisfaction with oneself (arrogantia). The former is called particularly *selfishness*: the latter *self-conceit* (p. 165).

But the new Imperative itself is not a consequence of any law but that of 'Nature', and it emerges from its elaborate wrapping of arguments as an exhortation pure and simple: no more and no less vulnerable than any other exhortation to embrace a principle. Kant concludes the *Foundations* reiterating that there *is* a moral Law which we are somehow both compelled to obey yet free to disobey, though admitting frankly at last that he cannot explain it:

> And thus while we do not comprehend the practical unconditional necessity of the moral Imperative, yet we comprehend its *incomprehensibility*; and this is all that can fairly be demanded of a philosophy which strives to carry its principles up to the very limit of human reason (p. 84).

As to that, we may be allowed to comment that though the moral Imperative admittedly makes an impressive barrier to the advance of human reason in the understanding of human aims and conduct, it is not in the nature of human reason to be halted for ever by even the most awe-inspiring phantoms.

II

We have seen that Kant's moral Will was only Good, not good, and that he insisted that a volition which is good, that is, benevolent or well-wishing, is not moral at all. This was a necessary consequence of the condition that Duty must have no aim, but Kant's personal views about the sort of motives people have are very significantly shown in various remarks he makes about human nature; and I think they throw much light on the *emotional* basis of his whole approach to the subject of human motives.

I quoted in section 3 above a statement to the effect that

some people may have such a disposition that they can 'take delight in the satisfaction of others so far as it is their own work.' Kant here seemed to overlook the possibility that people might take delight in the satisfaction of others even if it is not their own work; but we might think this is merely because he was writing here primarily about what people do, and not about their tastes. Elsewhere, however, there are plenty of indications that Kant viewed the majority of his fellows with a somewhat aloof eye. On Love to Men he has this to say:

> it is a Duty *to do good* to other men according to our power, whether we love them or not, and this Duty loses nothing of its weight, although we must make the sad remark that our species, alas! is not such as to be found particularly worthy of love when we know it more closely (p. 312).

In one of his earlier treatises we find this significant passage:

> Experience teaches us that a man normally views the happiness of other people with indifference: if he has himself furthered it, however, he is infinitely more pleased. The sufferings of other people usually leave a man equally indifferent: if he has caused them, however, they weigh much heavier upon him than if another had caused them.[1]

Although there are scattered references in other places to the possibility that a person may have an amiable disposition Kant says nothing which contradicts the view here expressed that few people care much about the happiness or the suffering of others, and that if they do try to promote the one or alleviate the other this is usually for the sake of impressing the onlooker. 'The opinion others may have of our worthiness, and their judgement on our actions, is a great motivating force, and one which coaxes from us many a sacrifice,[2] he says, after remarking that 'sympathy is not enough to excite the sluggish mind to activities for the common good'.

Kant, in short, did not believe that it is natural for men to care very much about what happens to their fellows; nor, apparently, did he regard this alleged natural callousness as being off-set by ideas of common advantage, which may lead

---

[1] *Kant's Sämmtliche Werke*, Hartenstein, VII–VIII, p. 616. (Trans. Teale in *Kantian Ethics*.)

[2] K.G.S., Vol. II, p. 218.

a sensible man to interest himself in the well-being of the group to which he belongs even if he happens to be completely hard-hearted. The desire to show off, we notice, produces 'many a sacrifice', in a context which seems to make sacrifice equivalent to good-doing. The idea that to do good might be expedient seems hardly ever to have occurred to him.

In Kant's view, then, people's desires or inclinations rarely lead them to do good, and this is because they are so selfish. They seek happiness, he says, but nowhere suggests that happiness can be enhanced by being shared. He speaks of friendship, it is true, but as part of his argument about the moral law; observing that even if there might never yet have been a sincere friend, 'pure sincerity in friendship' is required as a Duty (pp. 24–25).

The idea that the Moral Will must not be influenced in the smallest degree by any desire was conceived in a mind which seems to have taken it for granted that desires are pretty poor things, even when they are not actually malignant. Yet the very fact that the Moral Law is so often recommended as a corrective to harmful or hurtful human characteristics suggests that Kant himself was not devoid of benevolence; and we may think that it was benevolence which in fact partly accounted for the intrusion of Moralism into a system which as ethical theorist he was intent on keeping Pure—partly, though not entirely accounted for it, since without introducing veiled assumptions about benefit and harm, or in other words, without the help of basic values, Kant could have found no basis for his recommendations, over and above his intuitions about the purposes of Nature or God.

Kant seems often to be taking it as a matter of course that obedience to his moral Law would tend to produce behaviour which was good in the ordinary way, or at least less bad than most kinds of non-moral behaviour. For he was sure that the natural man was selfish, anti-social, and full of impure motives, which is to say full of motives. If the motives could be subjugated by morality the man would be Good, and in being so he would also be good. The Goodness was the condition for any really consistent goodness, *yet it could seldom if ever be attained.*

This pretty well amounted to a doctrine of despair, and Kant did not of course consistently believe it. He said, indeed, that it is doubtful whether a perfectly moral act has ever been performed: 'Although many things are done *in conformity* with what Duty prescribes, it is nevertheless always doubtful whether they are done strictly *from Duty* . . .' (p. 23). but elsewhere, as we have seen, argued that the moral Law is in our own nature and *compels* us to obey it.

One theme remains constant through all these uncertainties and contradictions: Kant's conviction that it is some way Better to act from a moral compulsion than because we *want* to do good. This notion is never explained, it is not even given a general statement in so many words, because it is taken entirely for granted. It is connected emotionally, we must suspect, with the idea that human desires are mostly evil—and also with the assumption that there is greater felicity in enjoying a sense of 'moral Worthiness' than in the knowledge of having done good; an assumption which is naïvely revealed in the following remark: 'We like to flatter ourselves by falsely taking credit for a more noble motive . . .' (p. 24), i.e. the moral Motive, not an ordinary one. (Kant's Pietistic upbringing may have been partly responsible for this attitude, and have implanted in his mind the idea that in order to do good one must sacrifice oneself—the cardinal principle of the Christian ethic, which is symbolized by the Cross.)

When Schiller complained that Kant was teaching that it is not moral to serve our friends if we enjoy doing so, and that according to Kant we ought to 'abhor' them, so that in benefiting them we can obey the moral law, Kant had no answer but to acknowledge that Duty *is* incompatible with pleasure: 'I admit that I cannot associate any *pleasantness* with the *conception of Duty*, just because of its dignity. For it involves unconditional obligation, which is directly contrary to pleasantness' (p. 330). He added, however, that if anyone asks whether the 'temperament of virtue' is 'spirited and cheerful, or anxiously depressed and dejected' it is hardly necessary to answer, for 'the latter slavish spirit can never exist without a secret *hatred* of the Law, and cheerfulness of heart in the performance of one's Duty is a mark of the genuineness of the virtuous disposition, without which one is never certain that he has *taken a liking* to good, that is to say, adopted it as his maxim' (p. 330). This description of the virtuous temperament makes one think irresistibly of a consciously conscientious person bustling about doing his Duty with a fixed resolute cheerfulness as genuinely gay as the smile of false teeth in a tumbler of sterilized water. Austere, rigorous, and joyless, Kant's ethic is permeated by the unhappy spirit of one who had little faith in spontaneous human goodness, and who did not even want to believe in it, because he had a deep distrust of *every* kind of spontaneity. His genuine dislike of the coercion of men by other men was matched by an almost obsessional preoccupation with the idea of self-coercion. We must force ourselves; compel ourselves; overcome every one of our natural desires. And to what end?

The Kant who had defended political freedom and who had said, 'There is nothing more dreadful than that the actions of a man should be subject to the will of another'[1] had an answer, albeit an indirect one, which he gave in the last chapter of the *Critique of Pure Reason*. At this time he had not yet embraced the idea that the moral Will is purely self-propelled, and he had just been proving the existence of God by the fact that we have moral compulsive feelings which must, he claimed, be infused into us by a supreme Lawgiver:

> We shall look upon ourselves as acting in conformity with the Divine Will only in so far as we hold sacred the Moral Law which Reason teaches us from the nature of actions themselves, and we shall believe that we can obey that Will only by promoting the weal (Wohl) of the universe in ourselves and others.[2]

This comes very near to saying that we must obey the moral Law because we think that so doing we shall be promoting, in conformity with the will of God, the advantage or well-being of man; and a shadow of this idea is also present in the doctrine that the *summum bonum* includes happiness as well as Virtue. But the Kant who insisted upon the unconditioned purity of the Moral Law could find no comprehensible answer to the question why we should subdue all our desires in order to obey it, for according to him Duty was an end in itself. In affirming this he was after all, and after so much, only reaffirming the central doctrine of pure Ethics regarding Duty, namely that, whatever it may be, it is our Duty to do it.

---

[1] Quoted by Russell in *A History of Western Philosophy*. Unfortunately neither Lord Russell nor I can now find the source of this quotation.

[2] *Critique of Pure Reason* (trans. Meiklejohn, p. 459).

12

It is hardly possible to overestimate the importance of Kant's contribution to ethical theory, though this importance has little to do with any of his prescriptive maxims—except in the oblique sense that by the very inconsistencies attending his attempts to lay down moral norms he demonstrated that not even *his* brilliant mind could in logic derive any recommendations for conduct from the Law of Pure Duty once he had laid it down. But Kant's truly great achievement was to draw, for the first time, a firm line of demarcation between ethical and non-ethical values, and it is one of the most perplexing oddities in the history of philosophy that the implications of this achievement have remained almost completely unexplored.

6

THE ETHICAL VALUES
OF BENTHAM

I ... discovered what was the really serious charge against him. It was no less than this, that he defined a 'good' man as a man who does good. This definition, as the reader will perceive at once if he is right-minded, is subversive of all true morality.

BERTRAND RUSSELL on Bentham.

SUMMARY: Bentham's ethical system, in the strongest possible contrast to Kant's, equates moral Goodness with beneficence. This example of Moralism, with its inevitable accompanying illogicalities, resulted from Bentham's ill-advised policy of trying to exalt his humane recommendations by endowing them with the 'absolute' authority of an ethical Imperative. If he had been content to eschew the ethical Ought and to argue for his reforms in terms of basic evaluation, by the light of human experience, he could have made Utilitarianism a self-consistent, non-ethical body of *advice* to men of good will and understanding.

I

To pass from Kantian to Benthamite Ethics is like emerging from an environment of monastic austerity and high-mindedness into the confident brightness of a well-lit department store.

Bentham was sure that this business of right and wrong, good and bad, was perfectly simple and straightforward. If we would only recognize that happiness—i.e. 'pleasure and the absence of pain' is necessarily pursued by everyone, and is therefore supremely good universally, we should see at once

H

that the promotion of his own and others' happiness and the reduction of his own and others' unhappiness are the best possible (the ultimately good *and* Good) activities for every human being.

Though the name Utilitarianism was first made famous by Bentham, he belonged to a school which had many exponents from the latter part of the eighteenth century, and the name is now used to cover such very various developments of the happiness doctrine as that of Helvetius, and that of John Stuart Mill.

Because the Utilitarians repudiated the idea of self-sacrifice as a Duty, and the doctrine of original sin, they were often reviled as Atheists, but in fact several leading members of the school supported their views with theological arguments. These helped to get over the inconvenient fact that benefiting others is not always strictly compatible with benefiting oneself. Thus John Gay maintained that though it is not always to our earthly advantage to do good, it is expedient in the long run because God, who wishes the sum of happiness to be increased, will reward those who promote it even at their own immediate expense, and punish those who diminish it for their own immediate advantage. In this way a man might perform prodigies of self-sacrifice and yet be obeying the dictates of Prudence.

Other exponents of the happiness-principle, notably Hume and Helvetius, dispensed with all supernatural authority for it, and Bentham developed his famous system under their influence and along their lines. He emphatically rejected any absolutist source for the idea of good. Other moral systems were hitched to a star called Perfection, God, or Nature. Benthamite Utilitarianism deliberately cut all cables and freed humanity from duties to anything but itself.

Bentham was deeply distrustful of supernaturalism as a foundation for principles of conduct; for he saw that once the claims of religion to ultimate ethical authority were conceded, even the most inhuman behaviour could be represented as morally Right: he saw that religion could be used to morally-justify *anything*; and so it was his deliberate purpose to formulate a moral system which should not only be more beneficent in its working than any founded on religion, but should be the only true and logically valid one in existence—an absolute barrier to any other because it alone could make use of 'moral' language in a logically consistent and meaningful way.

2

Bentham's main interest was to lay down theoretical foundations for a legal system to promote and safeguard the happiness of every single member of the community legislated for; the interests of each individual 'to count for one and no more than one'. The preservation of peace, the safeguarding of property, the control of vice—all these were of importance only in so far as they tended to the advantage of all those concerned.

Now this criterion was determined by *Bentham's own tastes*. He desired the happiness of men. As he himself might have said of another, his 'disposition' was 'good'; for 'good' meant 'tending to promote pleasure or reduce pain'. I think the critics of Utilitarianism, both favourable and unfavourable, have not sufficiently recognized that this benevolent bias underlies every version of the doctrine.[1] They are the less to blame because the Utilitarians themselves mostly failed to take account of it; though perhaps this was only natural, since like most practical thinkers they wanted to present their case as a rational conclusion based on dispassionately observed facts. All the same, it is a pity in more ways than one. For if the Utilitarians had noticed their own bias they could have used the example of themselves to show how the agent's own happiness may be *directly* promoted by promoting other people's. Further—and this applies particularly to Bentham's case—a great deal of dubious argumentation about motives would have turned out to be superfluous.

Bentham himself exposed the roots in passing, with some highly revealing remarks about the nature of justice, in the course of an argument directed to showing that if, as the orthodox claim, God is both good and just, his justice cannot run contrary to human happiness:

[1] But see Russell's comment in *The History of Western Philosophy*: 'If every man always pursued his own pleasure, how are we to secure that the legislator shall pursue the pleasure of mankind in general? Bentham's own instinctive benevolence (which his psychological theories prevented him from noticing) concealed the problem from him' (p. 805).

The religious sanction is founded, and can only be founded, on the moral attributes of God, and those moral attributes cannot oppose happiness.

Bentham then adds,

Justice is of use no farther than as the handmaid of benevolence. Justice is one of those means for compassing the ends that benevolence purposes.[1]

Here Bentham recognizes justice not as some impersonal ideal independent of human volitions, but as a structure designed to be 'the handmaid of benevolence'. In his view benevolence *comes first*, as a matter of course. I think the implications of this are very important. For in making justice itself subservient to benevolence Bentham actually points the way to that path which the Utilitarians could have followed consistently and profitably, avoiding all the pitfalls into which, to the great gratification of the less benevolent, they fell, because of their fatal insistence upon an ethical absoluteness for their system. (Gay and Paley did scramble over the pitfalls after a fashion, with a piece of theological dogmatism which critical minds were bound to reject—the evidence they adduced for an omnipotent Benevolence could so obviously be matched by evidence to the opposite effect. All that could really be said for their view was 'How nice it would be if they were right!')

In the isolated passage I have quoted, then, we find Bentham admitting tacitly that his interest in establishing a just legal system was that he wanted to give effect to 'the ends that benevolence purposes'—his own benevolence, and that of other like-minded people.

3

Utilitarianism was presented by Bentham not merely as an alternative to other ethical systems: it was to be demonstrably the only possible one. This claim is implied in many of his writings, for instance in the collected *Principles* where he says in one place that when interpreted in the Utilitarian sense 'the words "ought" and "right" and "wrong" and others of that stamp have a meaning: when otherwise they have none'. And

[1] *Deontology*, 1834 Edition, p. 117.

elsewhere he gives an example to prove that even moralists who think they are hostile to the principle of utility make use of utilitarian criteria themselves in the very act of giving reasons for rejecting them. People say, for example, that Utilitarianism is a *dangerous* principle.

> This is as much as to say, what? That it is not consonant to utility to consult utility: In short that it is *not* consulting it to consult it.[1]

This is a perfectly fair example of a typical muddle-headed attack upon Utilitarianism. Unfortunately it is not the only kind that can be made.

4

The most familiar comprehensive criticism of Utilitarianism is that in asserting that all men necessarily seek their own pleasure and avoid pain to themselves, and are incapable of doing any-thing else, it leaves no place for its moral imperatives, which are to be understood as 'You Ought to seek your own pleasure and avoid pain to yourself', and 'You Ought to promote the pleasure and combat the pain of others'.

Admittedly, if all oughts were ethical Oughts this criticism would be valid, but it is fair to consider whether the utilitarian 'ought' needs to be seen in this light at all. If not, then we might be able to rebut the criticism by showing that Utili-tarianism is not a strictly *ethical* system, but an *advisory* one.

Bentham introduces the word 'ought' in the very first para-graph of his *Principles* as follows:

> Nature has placed mankind under the governance of two sovereign masters, *pain* and *pleasure*. It is for them alone to point out what we ought to do, as well as to determine what we shall do. On the one hand the standard of right and wrong, on the other the chain of causes and effects, are fastened to their throne. They govern us in all we do, in all we say, in all we think: every effort we make to throw off our subjection will but serve to demonstrate and confirm it.[2]

---

[1] *A Fragment on Government, and An Introduction to the Principles of Morals and Legisla-tion* (Blackwell, 1946), p. 128.

[2] Op. cit., p. 125. (Contrast Bentham's reference to Nature with Kant's (Chapter 5, section 2 above); his Nature is metaphorical: Kant's has a *purpose*.)

What can Bentham have meant by saying that whilst
pleasure and pain *determine* what we shall do, they also point
out to us what we *ought* to do? Naturally if there were only
one meaning of 'ought', the strict moral meaning, Bentham's
statement would be very dubious, if not downright self-
contradictory. Many moralists have taken it for granted that
all oughts are essentially the same; but Kant, a strict moralist
if ever there was one—despite the lapses we have noted—knew
better, and in an early work he distinguished two types of ought
as follows:

> The word 'ought' [*sollen*] is capable of bearing two meanings,
> viz. I *ought* to do something (as a means) if I wish for some-
> thing else (as an end). Or, I ought directly [*unmittelbar*] to do
> something (as an end) and actualize it. The first *ought* could
> be called the necessity of means ... the second, the necessity
> of ends.[1]

It would be quite possible to regard the ought of Bentham's
opening sentence as standing for the means-to-end form, as
when we say, 'If you want this then you ought to do that'.
Perhaps to avoid ambiguity it would have been better if
Bentham had said not that it is for pleasure and pain to 'point
out' what we ought to do, but rather something to the effect
that pleasure and pain or the imagination of them are in the
last analysis what determines every course of action that we
decide to take for the realization of our aims. But at least there
is no ground for accusing him of self-contradiction on the
strength of this particular passage.

As to his use of 'right' and 'wrong': we might take it that he
is employing these, too, in the means-to-an-end sense, as in
'This is the right way to set about it', and 'You are holding
that thing at the wrong end'.

5

Now Bentham's statement clearly allows means-to-ends
considerations to be applied to the service of 'benevolent' or
'social' aims no less than to affairs of money-making and so
forth. Pleasure and pain determine 'the dictates of benevolence'
no less than other human dispositions, and on this view if people

[1] *Kant's gesammelte Schriften.* Ed. Berlin Academy, Vol. II, p. 298.

interested in justice choose to take trouble, and even voluntarily get into trouble, through their efforts to improve the law that is because, and only because, the balance of their pleasure-pain systems moves them in that direction. People often *do* try to benefit others, and, since everything they do is done in pursuit of pleasure or for the avoidance of pain, *a fortiori* these activities are simply part of the process of trying to get pleasure and avoid pain, so that in the context of a benevolent aim the *right* action is the action by the person who has the aim which is best fitted to serve that aim.

For example, if A's aim is to entertain B, who is a music-lover, and if in pursuit of this aim he takes B to a first-rate performance of works by his (B's) favourite composer, then we should say that A's action was right. And if, still with the aim of entertaining B, he takes him to an excruciatingly bad performance of the works, we should say that his action was wrong. But then according to this evaluation, if A's aim had been to give pain to B, taking him to the bad performance would have been the *right* thing to do, and on the other hand if he mistakenly supposed that B was bored stiff by classical music, though unwilling to admit it, and accordingly, his aim still being to give pain to B, took him to a fine performance of chamber music which B thoroughly enjoyed, we should have to say that A's action was, in the means-to-end sense, *wrong*.

There is no escaping the logic of this. If we are using 'right' and 'wrong' in the means-to-end sense, then the only rightness or wrongness that an action can have is that of furthering or obstructing the realization of a given aim of the agent's, which may be anything, from promoting world peace to poisoning his grandmother. This is the way we do constantly pass judgement on actions when we know their aim, when we are speaking non-ethically. Ethically speaking it is quite otherwise.

6

So far, Bentham's statement of his pleasure-pain principle does not require his 'ought', 'right', and 'wrong' to be taken in any other sense but that of the means-to-end. And in the same way it is possible to see his statement of the principle of utility as at least no more distinctively moral than, shall we say, an

ideological plan of campaign recommended to those who for
their own greater happiness want others to be happier, or less
unhappy.

The principle of utility which, Bentham says, 'recognizes'
our subjection to pain and pleasure, is set forth as follows:

> By the principle of utility is meant that principle which
> approves or disapproves of every action whatsoever according
> to the tendency which it appears to have to augment or
> diminish the happiness of the party whose interest is in ques-
> tion: or, what is the same thing in other words, to promote or
> to oppose that happiness. I say, of every action whatsoever, and
> therefore not only of every action of a private individual, but
> of every measure of government.[1]

Is this merely a concise statement of the 'benevolent' attitude
towards actions and institutions as they affect the hedonic state
of the people concerned, or is it something more?

It might be urged that the concepts of approval and disapproval which have now been introduced place the principle
of utility in the class of strict ethics, but in fact I do not see
that approval and disapproval are *necessarily* moral attitudes.
They might be regarded merely as *forms* of liking and dislike,
such as we may feel towards, say, a way of behaving or thinking.
If we disapprove of such things that may be only because of a
feeling that they show, or are likely to promote, a tendency
that for one reason or another we think of with anxiety or distaste; and on the same view, when we approve of something
we imagine it conduces to a trend which we want to see
promoted, or counters something we dislike in a general way.
Also approval and disapproval are decidedly' exhibitionist'
attitudes. There is not much point, perhaps, in approving or
disapproving of anything unless we show that we do so, and
because of their consistency, because they are dominant over
more ephemeral feelings, and also because of their open, social
character, approval and disapproval are suitable attitudes to
determine a *policy*, which might be taken to be Bentham's
object here. In saying that the 'principle of utility' approves
and disapproves, he need have meant no more than that the
Utilitarian approves and disapproves, and have been saying in
effect, 'Let those who want the increase of felicity determine

[1] *Op. cit.*, p. 126.

and declare that they approve of everything which tends in this direction and disapprove of everything which tends in the opposite one.'

Notice that Bentham has not suggested in this place that everybody must acknowledge the principle of utility. Indeed it seems clear that a person whose pleasure-pain system does not produce in him a general disapproval of unhappiness and approval of happiness cannot possibly subscribe to it.

Bentham both affirms his principle, implying that it is in fact adhered to by some people at least, and also *advocates* it by his proposal that they, the benevolent, should recognize it and deliberately refer to it for the solution of all human problems, implying that their efforts are more likely to be successful if they do; in other words, that this will be the right course for them to follow.

7

So far it has been possible to defend Utilitarianism against the particular charge of illogically trying to derive ethical maxims from a determinist principle, by showing that the 'ought', 'right', and 'wrong' of Bentham's initial statement of his principle are not necessarily to be taken as moral at all; but of course it has been apparent from the first that this could only be a rear-guard action, and that the end must come soon. It comes with the following elaboration of the statement of the Principle quoted above, taken in conjunction with another statement which I shall quote afterwards:

> Of an action that is conformable to the principle of utility one may always say either that it is one that ought to be done, or at least that it is not one that ought not to be done. One may say also, that it is right it should be done: at least that it is not wrong it should be done: that it is a right action: at least that it is not a wrong action.[1]

Then follows the claim that 'ought', 'right', and 'wrong' only have a meaning when interpreted in this sense.

Now if we could take the 'one' of 'one may say . . .' to stand for a Utilitarian we might take Bentham to be only saying in effect that when Utilitarians use these terms about actions they

[1] Op. cit. p. 127.

mean only that they approve of them, no more and no less.
And the assertion that 'ought', 'right', and 'wrong' only have
a meaning when used in this way might perhaps be dismissed
as a rather over-emphatic comment on the muddled use of these
terms by conventional moralists. But in the light of the
following passage, which consists of an imaginary conversation
between Bentham the Utilitarian and a non-Utilitarian, this
interpretation is seen to be quite out of the question.

'I feel in myself,' say you, 'a disposition to approve of such or
such an action is a moral view: but this is not owing to any
notion I have of its being an useful one to the community. I do
not pretend to know whether it be an useful one or not: it may
be, for aught I know, a mischievous one'. 'But is it then', say I,
'a mischievous one? Examine; and if you can make yourself
sensible that it is so, then, if duty means anything—that is, moral
duty—it is your *duty* at least to abstain from it: and more than
that—if it is what lies in your power, and can be done without
too great a sacrifice—to endeavour to prevent it. It is not your
cherishing the notion in your bosom, and giving it the name of
virtue, that will excuse you.'

'I feel in myself,' say you again, 'a disposition to detest such
and such an action in a moral view; but this is not owing to
any notion I have of its being a mischievous one to the community. I do not pretend to know whether it be a mischievous
one or not: it may not be a mischievous one; it may be, for
aught I know, an useful one'. 'May it indeed,' say I, 'be an
useful one? But let me tell you then, that unless duty, and right
and wrong, be just what you please to make them, if it really
be not a mischievous one, and anybody has a mind to do it,
it is no duty of yours, but on the contrary it would be very
wrong in you, to take upon you to prevent him: detest it within
yourself as much as you please . . . but if you go about, by word
or deed, to do anything to hinder him, or make him suffer for
it, it is you, and not he, that have done wrong . . .'[1]

Bentham has now revealed himself as a true Ethicist, for in
this dialogue he is straightforwardly opposing one set of moral
criteria to another set. He is telling a man of one ethical per-
suasion—the Intuitionist—that he Ought to abandon his standpoint, and that it is Wrong in him to do this which he thinks
Right, and that it would be Right in him to do that which he

[1] Op. cit. p. 143 n.

thinks Wrong. This is moral exhortation, and Bentham's ought, right and wrong as here used demand capital letters, or as spoken aloud, a reverent tone of voice, for they are categorical: like Kant's Categorical Imperative they are '*a priori*'.

8

What could Bentham have answered if his interlocutor in the dialogue had retorted—adopting *ad hoc* a utilitarian standpoint —'Why should I not try to prevent such or such an action from being performed, if that action would give great spiritual pain to me and only a little pleasure to the agent?' The only possible answer consistent with the position Bentham had now openly adopted would have been that it is absolutely Wrong to prevent a man from performing an action that he wants to perform if it is not 'a mischievous one to the community'. So we must now recognize the phrase 'It is right it should be done' and similar ones in the earlier quotation as representing true moral maxims, as their form would, after all, lead us to expect.

To say of an action that it Ought to be done, or that it is Right it should be done is entirely different from saying that it is in the circumstances the right thing to do. The latter merely implies that, given the aim and the circumstances, the contemplated action is, in the speaker's judgement, the one most likely to be successful; and unless it is an Ethicist who speaks, there is no sense at all in speaking of a right or wrong method, or policy, or legal system, or anything else of the kind, unless it is understood what is being aimed at.

It is one thing to say, 'For those who want to promote general happiness it is always right to act in *this* sort of way, and wrong to act in *that* sort of way', and quite another thing to say 'It is always right that happiness should be promoted', for in this sentence 'right' can only mean 'Right'.

It is worth while pausing to consider what has really happened to the argument at this crucial stage. If we are not to accuse Bentham of deliberate artfulness, then we must assume that he really believed he had succeeded in pinning down the moral Ought with the brass tacks of his principle of utility. By what process of reasoning, then, was he able to satisfy himself that he had done this?

All his subsequent development of the Utilitarian doctrine shows that Bentham thought he had been able to derive a *universal aim* from his pleasure-pain theory. Now if this really had been so the rest would have followed. For then the individual's aim-determined 'right' and 'wrong' would have been universalized.

Everybody, says Bentham in effect, seeks pleasure and avoids pain. This means that the increase of pleasure, or the reduction of pain (according to circumstances) is a universal aim. The right method for achieving an aim is the one which effectively promotes, or brings about, its realization. The wrong method is one that prevents or obstructs its realization. Therefore every voluntary action—which is to say every attempt at pleasure-increase or pain-reduction—which is effective must be called right, in conformity with this usage; and every action—which still means every attempt at pleasure-increase or pain-reduction —which is misguided (i.e. which does not conduce to the universally sought end) must be called wrong. Or alternatively, we could say that the one ought to be performed and the other ought not.

This, I think, is a fair statement of the main substance of the argument.

The defect of this reasoning, as rival moralists are never tired of pointing out, is that even if it is true to say that everybody always aims at pleasure and pain-avoidance *for himself* this is not the same as saying that he aims at the total increase of pleasure or the total reduction of pain, since he might be prepared to increase his own pleasure at the price of somebody else's, or reduce his own pain by increasing the pain of others. Of course, if the interests of all men were so closely integrated that in effectively pursuing pleasure for himself each person, whether intentionally or not, were necessarily thereby increasing the sum total of pleasure in the world, then indeed we might say that though he may not be consciously promoting a universally-shared aim, it makes no *practical* difference; so that if an action is right for him it is, in view of the universal aim, universally 'right it should be done'. But Bentham could not really have believed in a state of affairs so obviously at variance with the facts of existence: he was perfectly well aware that people are in the habit of benefiting themselves at each other's expense, and part of his interest as a benevolent legislator was to alter the conditions which fostered that practice.

One has only to read the attacks of other Ethicists to see how in his very attempts to disarm his morally-minded opponents Bentham succeeded in disarming himself. By meeting the enemy on their own ground he delivered himself into their hands.

A typical instance of the sort of criticism Bentham 'asked for' by his attempt to adapt the moral Ought to his own ends occurs in the Introduction to the 1948 edition of the *Principles* by Wilfred Harrison, on the whole a favourably disposed critic. In reference to Bentham's 'ought' he says, 'If pleasure is that at which we unavoidably aim, then there is no question of what we ought to do.'[1]

This might have seemed as inept as saying, 'If somebody wants to become a millionaire, then there is no question of what he ought to do to attain this end.' But unluckily, because Bentham has allowed his advisory ought to swell into the Ought of the ethical imperative, the criticism must be allowed to be valid; for *this* 'ought' requires us to *overrule* the pleasure-pain principle.

Naturally, it is fairly obvious why Bentham found he had to adopt an ethical position. Mere recognition of the pleasure-pain principle could not by itself be made the basis of an argument either for benevolent intentions or for beneficent actions. Something else was requisite, after the facts of human motivation as he saw them had been noted, to lend force to his humane recommendations, and Bentham, unhappily for his thesis, saw no alternative but to construct an ethical scheme which, though it could not be derived from the pleasure-pain principle, could at least be hitched to it after a fashion with arguments employing terms which happen to belong to both ethical and non-ethical discourse, treating them as moral and meaningful only in one sense—the Utilitarian sense.

9

Bentham's analysis of motives is not, on the whole, very valuable. What is chiefly remembered is his challenging pronouncement,

[1] Op. cit., p. L.

'*There is no such thing as any sort of motive that is in itself a bad one.*[1] This he elaborates as follows:

> Let a man's motive be ill-will, call it even malice, envy, cruelty: it is still a kind of pleasure that is his motive; the pleasure he takes at the thought of the pain which he sees, or expects to see, his adversary undergo. Now even this wretched pleasure, taken by itself, is good . . . [While] it lasts and before any bad consequences arise, it is as good as any other that is not more intense.'

This rather unnerving example is, of course, only a ruthless underlining of the point, trivial in Bentham's context, that nobody can wish to do anything but good *to himself*. Perhaps, also, Bentham was especially concerned here to exclude the use of 'bad', as applied to motives, to stand for 'selfish' or anything of the kind which does not strictly confine the meaning to 'pleasure-averting', or 'pain-promoting'. Once he is satisfied that he has disposed of all claims to a special kind of Goodness or Badness for motives he tactily admits that they can be good or bad in the same way as other things, that is, 'Good on account of their tendency to produce pleasure, or avert pain, bad on account of their tendency to produce pain or avert pleasure.'

It is often difficult to know whether Bentham, when he is discussing motives, is using 'good' and 'bad' as they are ordinarily used, or in his own ethical sense, and one sometimes gets the impression that he is not always sure himself. If he had consistently applied 'good' to intentions and volitions in precisely the same way that he applies it to everything else, he could never have made 'good-will' just one item in a list of 'motives' which he later draws up, classifying them severally as Social, Semi-social, and Self-regarding. Seeing that he has previously insisted over and over again that *all* motives are necessarily self-regarding it is really most disconcerting to find 'good-will' (thus hyphenated) being classified among 'purely social motives'.

Was this a slip? Alas, no: for at the end of the list we find this comment on the 'semi-social' group, (which includes 'the love of reputation, the desire of amity, and the motive of religion'): 'Indeed these last, social as they may be termed,

[1] Op. cit., p. 218.

are self-regarding at the same time,[1] which inevitably implies that the 'purely social' motives in the list are *not* self-regarding. Surely Hume was right when he said:

> Whatever contradiction may vulgarly be supposed between the *selfish* and *social* sentiments and dispositions, they are really no more opposite than selfish and ambitious, selfish and revengeful, selfish and vain.[2]

10

Why, one wonders, should Bentham, contradicting so much of what he had said elsewhere, have gone out of his way at this point to divorce self-regarding motives from motives which are socially orientated, making them a different *class* of motive? Bentham of all people, who could declare with blythe optimism, 'There are no occasions on which a man has not some motives for consulting the happiness of other men'. Can a good 'will' or good intentions be 'pure' in the Kantian sense? Why should they be?

Perhaps the truth of the matter is that Bentham was betrayed into inconsistency by his very objection to the way that the transcendentalists applied 'good' and 'bad' to motives. He saw that on their lips these terms had no necessary connection with any hedonic considerations whatsoever, and he therefore tried to find a mode of approach to the subject of motives which should not overlap with theirs at any point. But instead of using the popular conception of motives as 'reasons' or types of reason for our actions, and then consistently opposing a Utilitarian evaluation of their goodness or badness to other existing ones he chose the fatal course of adapting the idea of motive itself to the exigencies of his thesis. Thus again we see how Utilitarianism, launched on a game of hide-and-seek with the Absolute, ends by falling headlong into its lap.

In non-ethical discourse what we mean by a good motive is, quite consistently, a benevolent motive, or one with a beneficent tendency. In saying that a man's motive was good we mean that he intended or purposed to do good by his action, and this regardless of whether or not he expected to derive

[1] Op. cit., p. 236.
[2] *Inquiry Concerning the Principles of Morals*, (Ed. Open Court Publishing Co.), p. 121.

material, as distinct from emotional, advantage from it. And
if we say that somebody's motive was bad we mean that he
intended to do harm, or that the sort of action resulting from
the motive would be likely to be harmful. Bentham endorsed
this view of the matter in many places, yet for all that, he never
retracted his disastrous assertion that there can be no such
thing as a bad motive, and tripped over it repeatedly.

It is interesting to compare Bentham's equivocations over
motives with Kant's very similar proceedings with the concept
of 'will'. Though they started at opposite poles in their view
of the nature of morality, their arguments eventually foundered
in the same logical morass.

Kant, though favouring good behaviour in the non-ethical
sense, wanted to preserve his Categorical Imperative from all
contamination by desire for anything at all, and so, struggle
as he might and did through whole chapters of elaborate exposition and statement and restatement there could be no
escaping the débâcle: his moral Will was purposeless. Bentham
for his part wanted to preserve his 'ought' from all transcendent
associations and *yet* keep its imperative character (see the
quotation in section 4 above), so his motives had to be always
good and yet sometimes Bad, i.e., such that they Ought not to
be implemented. For Kant, hemmed in by the stone walls of
his uncompromising apriorism there could be no escape from
the ultimate collapse of his thesis in a welter of self-contradictions and double meanings; but in Bentham's case one feels
that he need only have taken one decisive step away from the
moralistic path to have achieved his aim: a rational philosophy
of conduct free from metaphysics and conveying sound *advice*
to all those capable of entertaining the idea of *collective* advantage—that is to the vast majority of human beings—effectively
serving, in his own phrase, 'the purposes of benevolence'.

11

The Utilitarians were convinced that enlightened self-interest
is more effective in making men good than any pretence that
they can only do good in the process of attempting, as it were,
to stab themselves in the back; and there are reasons based
on experience for thinking they were right. But both their

theory of conduct and their advice are fatally weakened by the ethical case that they felt bound to argue, even though a great deal of what they said logically implied rejection of it. If Bentham had said that he was presenting his Utilitarianism as an *alternative* to morality, and explained that his 'good' was non-ethical and 'Oughtless'; that his advice was no more ethical than the advice in a cookery-book; and if he had stated at the outset what he did indeed now and then imply, that he was addressing only those who, whatever their reasons, wanted mankind to be happier, or less unhappy, his position would have been logically invulnerable.

As it was, Bentham laid himself open to refutation both by the malevolent—who knew quite well, and loudly proclaimed, that the very last thing some people want is for others to be happy—and also by the Ethicists, whether malevolent or not, who pointed out that the pleasure-pain principle, if valid, left no place for the *Duty* of goodness to others.

Bentham held on to the idea of moral obligation even in the teeth of his own insistence on the neglected necessary truth that we are incapable of acting voluntarily against our will. Once embarked on this fatal course there could be no turning back: Utilitarianism could never be established as a self-consistent system of thought, and it only remained for John Stuart Mill to complete the demonstration by his famous dictum that it is sometimes our Duty to sacrifice our greatest good for the good of others.

12

Why did the enlightened and liberal-minded thinkers of the later eighteenth and early nineteenth centuries feel it necessary to cling to the categorical Ought even at the price of stultifying their own psychological premise? True, they were only keeping up the traditional practice of couching recommendations about conduct in the language of metaphysical ultimates, but in the case of the Utilitarians this can hardly be the whole story. The fact is that the *gap* between their theory of motive and their prescriptions for promoting human happiness was there, and had to be filled in somehow.

Looking at their doctrines now in the light of present-day

ideas, it may strike us that if they had brought to the help of their thesis certain psychological considerations on the one hand, and economic considerations on the other, the gap would not have yawned so wide. One fact of psychology Bentham at least might have made much greater use of:

Everyone knows how largely our actions are influenced by our desire to live up to a personal ideal. Most people are affected for a large part of their lives by the desire to be different in this way or that: to *be*, not only to *appear*, say, 'tougher', or kinder than they are, or simply to be in a general way more like the people they admire. No 'sense of Duty' is involved in the efforts we make to transform ourselves into the kind of persons we wish to be: the personal ideal is a potent motive-force in its own right. We might say in Bentham's phrase that it belongs to our pursuit of 'the pleasures of self-esteem', only that there is so much attempted paid-avoidance about it! 'That we may be dissatisfied with ourselves,' wrote Schopenhauer, 'and saddened by reason of sufferings which we have inflicted, not undergone, is a plain fact, and impossible to be denied.' Being dissatisfied with ourselves or contemptuous of our own behaviour is acutely painful, and so we make great efforts to avoid that pain, even to the length of trying to alter our own desires and propensities—in which, astonishingly, we are sometimes successful.

Evidently the kind of personal ideal we set up for ourselves is largely, though by no means always entirely, determined by the sort of personal qualities which are generally admired in the social group to which we belong, even though they may not be the ones we are accustomed to praise openly. Thus in a society in which women are apt to be despised, gentleness, sympathy for suffering, and dislike of violence tend also to be despised, for all that we call them virtues, because owing to early childhood impressions these dispositions are universally associated with women (even though they may be conspicuously lacking in particular cases), and so boys, and not seldom girls as well, admire roughness and toughness and try to develop these qualities in themselves, as the opposite to womanish gentleness. (I do not know what the remedy would be, but this is surely a feature of our cultural pattern that is worth the attention of educators with a humane bias.) If it were possible to encourage a general *admiration* for tenderness and imaginative sympathy for others these qualities would be more in evidence than they are now; and if, on the other hand, brutality were regarded with *contempt* people would tend to become ashamed of this tendency in themselves and would try to overcome it.

The Utilitarians knew that people can be kind, and they also realized that, the human will being extremely potent, good will might be a most effective agency of human good; but perhaps they failed to give enough attention to the possibilities of improving methods for cultivating it.

13

Another factor making for good which again is totally unconnected with the sense of Duty is that discomfort which very many people feel at the sight or imagination of others' sufferings, and which was characteristic of the Utilitarians themselves. Whether from mistaken modesty or some other obscure cause the Utilitarians gave surprisingly little weight to this socially valuable quality. Helvetius in particular almost entirely neglected it in his account of motives. We are all selfish, he declared, and selfishness is nothing to be ashamed of. Well and good: our self-centred activities if intelligently directed often conduce to the community's advantage. This is quite true, but it is undoubtedly also true that the total effect of the most devoted self-seeking may produce, quite wittingly, far more suffering than happiness, and would do so more often than it does if it were not for the faculty of sympathy, which is a vital ingredient of good will, and one which can be cultivated, especially in children. If we have good will ourselves we shall want to promote it in others, and here early influences and education can do much, even though it may be true that at a certain level of misery the desire to relieve one's own suffering will always be stronger than the desire to relieve anyone else's.

14

This brings us to the second group of facts about humanity which, from the opposite side, as it were, of the Utilitarian 'gap' could have helped to close it up.

Bentham had little that was new to say about the economic aspect of things as affecting human inter-relations and conduct generally. This was perhaps because he thought mainly in terms of government. His ideal government, though democratically elected, was of the paternal rather than the democratic pattern and its function was to make and preserve good laws. It it did not carry out this function, and so became intolerable, it could and should, he said, be overthrown; but apparently only in favour of another that should be a better, more benign and just, parent to its subjects. He was deeply interested in, and sympathetic to, the new American Constitution, but one feels that the idea of government by the people for the people was not carried very far in his mind. In the same way, he favoured social justice in terms of the master-and-man relationship, and he accepted the division of society into rich and poor as a matter of course. Nor did he shrink from noting that this state of things must inevitably mean a basic conflict of interests. Thus he wrote:

> The unequal gifts of nature and of fortune will always create jealousies: there will always be opposition of interests, and, consequently, rivalries and hatred. Pleasures will be purchased by pains, enjoyment by privations. Painful labour, daily subjection, a condition near allied to indigence, will always be the lot of numbers.[1]

In face of this outspoken recognition of the existence of opposed interests it seems odd that in the role of utilitarian theorist Bentham could say, speaking about the relationship between sovereign and people:

> But the good of the community is the sum of the several particular *goods* . . . of the several individuals of which it is composed, so that to augment the good of any one such individual is *pro tanto* to augment the good of the whole community. A law therefore of which the immediate end is no other than the good of the person whose law it is does not on that account cease to be such a law as is capable of being warranted by the principle of utility . . .[2]

Farther on he remarks, however,

---

[1] *Benthamiana.* Ed. J. H. Burton. p. 103 (*Perfectibility of the Law Chimerical*).
[2] *Limits of Jurisprudence Defined* (Columbia U.P.), p. 113–14.

. . . as to the sovereign, the end or external motive he can have
had in view in adopting [a] . . . law, can upon the principle
of utility, have been no other than the greatest good of the
community; which end we suppose his measures to be directed
to of course: since it is only in as far as that is the case that
these enquiries are calculated or designed to be of any use
to him.[1]

This, on a favourable view, corrects the dubiousness of the
argument about the advantage of the 'One' being conducive
to that of the many, for it now transpires that Bentham was
writing of Utilitarian-minded sovereigns only, whose 'good'
would never be enjoyed at their subjects' expense, or at least
not intentionally. This explanation substantially narrows the
scope of the argument; but then the narrowness was really
inherent in its very terms. For to say that augmenting the good
of one person, the sovereign, *necessarily* augments the good of
the community because he forms a part of it would have been
like saying that to augment the contents of the top drawer of
a chest of drawers is necessarily to augment the contents of the
whole, whilst ignoring the fact that it could be done simply
by transferring clothes to it from the lower drawers. It seems
hardly possible that Bentham could have meant to make use of
such an absurd argument.

I feel I have been doing my best for Bentham here, but
seeing how frequently he refers to the conflict of interests, and
seeing also what was his attitude towards the execution of
Charles I, it seems fair to give him the benefit of the doubt in
the present instance. A Benthamite monarch would certainly
not want to benefit at the expense of his subjects; even so,
with all the good will in the world he might find it hard to
avoid doing so under a social system which worked dispropor-
tionately in his favour.

15

In his more general observations Bentham did not say in so
many words that he was addressing only those members of
the privileged classes who were out to promote the greatest
happiness of the greatest possible number, but here too he

[1] Op. cit., p. 114.

seems to have been taking it for granted that his ideas could only be expected to influence those who were *already* well-disposed. Seeing that the mere existence of these men of good will in the ruling class hadn't been enough to bring about the social improvements Bentham wished to see, it seems as if his purpose in regard to them must have been to reinforce their natural benevolence by presenting them with the greatest-happiness principle as a practical guide.

Always provided that the benevolence was strong enough as a motive, and provided also that the benevolent were numerous enough and influential enough, this might have been sufficient to bring about the moderate improvements in the lot of the majority which Bentham then felt to be feasible; but in fact he did not himself believe that placing the principle of utility in the hands of the better sort of rulers would be enough, without the reinforcement of an ethical doctrine whose pressure should be felt even by those who were *not* naturally very benevolent. He knew very well that there were powerful persons whose pleasure-pain systems directed them to disregard the greatest-happiness principle, but he believed, apparently, that some of them might be intimidated into better courses by a moral doctrine which had the effect of condemning their parasitism as Wrong.

We may think that what would have been very much more effective would have been to convince the majority of the nation that the conditions under which a few people could thrive so egregiously at their expense were not inevitable and might be changed, and to suggest the means for making the changes. In this way the gap between the Utilitarian theory of motives and the ends recommended for their satisfaction would have been filled in, not by moral exhortations, but by practical advice. But Bentham, in fact, had almost nothing to say to the exploited themselves, nor, on the other hand, did he expect the ruling classes, however benevolent, to quarrel with their caviar to the extent of encouraging revolutionary movements.

This being the position, it certainly might seem that there was something to be said for the backing up of humane counsels by such utilitarian maxims as 'The obligation to minister to general happiness is an obligation paramount to, and inclusive of, every other.'

An advantage of this from the humane point of view was that once such principles had been enunciated it was difficult for anybody to repudiate them openly, unless, of course, on religious grounds. The chief disadvantage from the point of view of Utilitarian theory was that it involved virtually reinstating the previously rejected assumption that people are capable of acting from disinterested or purely moral motives —if 'obligation' meant anything at all.

As regards the former point, it is at least an open question whether the ethical formulation was any more awkward to reject than would have been some non-ethical statement which simply *offered* to rulers the general legislative aim of promoting happiness as an alternative to any other aim, and publicly saying to them 'choose'. But in either case the ruler's words would not necessarily have been followed by deeds, and religion, as always, was at hand to provide 'moral' counterblasts to proposals which were felt to err on the side of liberalism.

Unfortunately even Utilitarianism itself, given a slight twist, and with the aid of selected Benthamite texts, could be, and was, used for the same sort of ends. 'The interest of the community is the sum of the interests of the several members who compose it.' Right. So by increasing the 'national prosperity' we really benefit all round, and we must not lose sight of this great truth because in the process thousands of small children have, regrettably, to be worked to death in the mills and mines. Hardboiled intellectuals like Herbert Spencer, and soft-headed geese like Harriet Martineau both subscribed to this faith which must have made the kindly Bentham turn in his grave.

16

Bentham's doctrines were sincerely intended to serve 'the purposes of benevolence', but the pity of it was that to him this meant only, or mainly, the kind of benevolence which the strong may (or may not) feel towards the weak, and not the spontaneous good will which is engendered among people united in common aims, and with coinciding interests.

As one might have expected any Utilitarian to recognize, the latter sort of good will has always proved the strongest and most effective in improving the human lot, besides propagating

general good will itself as a normal and reasonable attitude of
mind.

*If citizens could not procure their own private happiness without
promoting that of the public, there would be none vicious but fools.*

Thus Helvetius, penetrating to the very heart of the matter.
Good will has always existed in rough ratio to community of
interests. Therefore if we want more good will in the world—
and there are sound practical reasons for wanting it, whether or
not we have reasons of sentiment as well—we shall work to
promote conditions under which it becomes ever less easy for
people to procure their own private happiness at others'
expense. With this aim in view we should have no need of
moral maxims to bolster up benevolence: they would be completely out of place.

But if we are not like this; if through greed or stupidity or
lack of sympathetic imagination we are indifferent to the
welfare of anybody but ourselves and our families, then if we
want the support of a morality to justify our mode of thought
and way of life, Utilitarianism will naturally be the very last
to attract us. After all, there are plenty of other moralities,
some of them eminently suitable for the vindication of an
anti-social attitude, and with a firm foundation of religious
dogma as a safeguard against the assaults of reason.

17

What sort of person, then, was left to be influenced by the
Utilitarian creed in the direction the Utilitarians desired?

The answer, I think, is, the benevolent but muddled; and in
particular those who had been brought up to accept Christianity
as the only source and inspiration of good will and good action.
Utilitarianism confronted them with the refreshing and liberat-
ing proposition that goodness is human, whether or not it is
also divine, and that there is nothing inherently evil about self-
regard. This was a valuable lesson, even though it did not go
far enough in disentangling thought from the paradoxes of
religio-moralism, and went too far in its sanguine presumption
that self-regard usually works automatically for the general
advantage, whatever the surrounding conditions may be. To

say that it is our Duty to promote happiness is really not to say anything very significant. To say that in promoting our own happiness we always, or nearly always, promote that of the community is unfortunately to contradict the facts. What we *can* say, in the spirit of Utilitarianism, is that those of us who really want mankind to become less wretched ('happier' has an ironical sound in view of the prevailing state of things) will do well to recognize that *conflict of interests* is the chief obstacle to this development, and try to do something about it.

18

To sum up: The attempts of the Utilitarians to set up a moral system on a foundation of facts about human desires was a failure: inevitably, since no moral maxim can be derived from a statement of fact. (In the conclusion of a syllogism no term can occur which has not occurred in one of the premises.) In its aspect as advice to the benevolent in the ruling class Utilitarianism was certainly very helpful in providing them with a consistent guiding principle for the pursuit of certain limited objectives. Benthamite Utilitarianism performed the important service of demonstrating that in order to be good it is not necessary to be either pious or unselfish, but retreated from the conclusion that it is not necessary to be moral either; and by trying to convert Ethics to its own purposes stultified those very premises—the pleasure-pain principle—on which it claimed to be based.

This could have been avoided if, on the one hand, the idea of benevolence had been widened and made the basis of an inquiry into the best methods of cultivating it both as an emotional attitude and as a 'motive' arising from practical considerations and if, on the other hand, there had been willingness to think in terms of a possible social order under which it would no longer be appropriate to plead for good will from one section of the community towards the other, though inappropriate to plead for it from the other towards the first. (In our own day some progress in this direction has already been made here and there. In the middle of the nineteenth century it would not have been surprising to hear a benevolent person exhorting employers to be kinder to factory-workers.

Nowadays the factory-workers are sometimes urged to be kinder to their employers, the community, and thereby also to themselves. This is much more in line with Utilitarianism, non-ethically considered; for we associate our pleas to the workers with counsels of expediency. It would not be at all a good plan to adorn them with exhortations about the beauty or the duty of self-sacrifice.)

As a system of advice to men of good intentions, or of potential good intentions, Utilitarianism could have been propounded, consistently with Bentham's purposes, roughly like this: It is human nature to seek happiness and avoid unhappiness, but though the hedonic interests of men sometimes harmonize, they also often clash. Where interests harmonize men tend to promote each other's happiness, and vice versa. Accordingly it is to the advantage of those who for their own happiness want a *general* increase of happiness and reduction of unhappiness to promote conditions under which interests do *not* clash—or in other words, it is to their advantage to promote universal social justice.

7

THE ETHICAL VALUES
OF G. E. MOORE

> Hold thou the good: define it well;
> For fear divine Philosophy
> Should push beyond her mark, and be
> Procuress to the Lords of Hell.
>
> TENNYSON

SUMMARY: *Principia Ethica* is chiefly an exercise in the analysis of the word and the concept 'good'. Moore asserts that GOOD is an indefinable object for which the word 'good' stands, though at the same time the *adjective* 'good' is applicable to a number of things in judgements which are, he pronounces, 'in the vast majority of cases ethical judgements'. This work has been a fertile source of confused thinking on the subject of evaluation.

I

Moore's famous *Principia Ethica*,[1] first published in 1903, and reissued without alteration in 1922, with various reprints up to 1960, is still considered to be one of the most important contributions to ethical theory published this century. On its first appearance *Principia Ethica* was enthusiastically received on account of the fresh impulse it gave to ethical philosophy. It

[1] Although I know that Moore later revised some of his opinions—in particular with respect to the relations of the terms 'good' and 'right'—I am for convenience restricting the present discussion to this one work, Moore's ethical *magnum opus*. I feel this is justified by Moore's note to the 1922 edition of *Principia Ethica*, published ten years later than the shorter work called *Ethics*, in which he says, 'This book . . . is reprinted because I am still in agreement with its main tendency and conclusions.'

opened up new fields for exploration and cultivation at a time when it was felt that the old ones had been worked over and over until their fertility was quite exhausted.

Throughout the nineteenth century a widening rift had been developing between two leading ethical schools in Britain. On the one side stood the absolutists and intuitionists who emphasized, in the words of Martineau, 'the pervading consciousness of higher authority'—a consciousness which Butler had called 'conscience' and Hutcheson 'the moral sense'. On the other side, inspired by the humanism of Helvetius, Hume, and Bentham, the practical, down-to-earth Utilitarians seemed to be taking a path away from absolutism and the categorical, towards a standpoint which made 'Ethics' consist mainly of a set of useful principles for the benevolent to follow in pursuit of their aim of improving the human lot, and all but ignored the unqualified moral Ought insisted upon by the strict Ethicists. It is not difficult to imagine that Utilitarianism could soon have evolved into a plain theory of aims and conduct consisting on the practical side of advice to men of good will on the best way to bring about the social reforms they favoured: advice hardly more 'moral' than that contained in *The Vegetable-Grower's Handbook*.

But as it turned out, there was to be no such future for Utilitarianism; indeed no future at all. No dramatic clash with the Absolutists, no decisive break-away ever occurred, and the surviving vestiges of Bentham's creed, already disintegrating under the anxious qualifications of John Stuart Mill, faded away in the rarefied yet stimulating atmosphere of the new Idealism, whose prophet was G. E. Moore.

To the group of young Cambridge intellectuals who made *Principia Ethica* their Bible, Moore's claim for the supreme worth of friendship and the beautiful came as a happy release from the rather arid pleasure-pain calculations of Bentham. Yet at the same time, the change of approach was not so drastic as to repel those whose social consciences had developed under the influence of Bentham and Mill; for the new Ethic did not call for any denial of the just claims of social obligation: it merely played them down. As J. M. Keynes, an early devotee, put it, 'Moore . . . had one foot on the threshold of the new Heaven, but the other foot in Sidgwick, and the Benthamite calculus, and the general rules of correct behaviour.'[1]

Many a lesser Moralist has come to grief through trying to stand with one foot on terra firma and the other up in the clouds; but not so the young Professor Moore, who in performing this feat maintained his balance with the aid of one Word: a word of such unexampled elasticity that throughout the ages it had stretched all the way between Heaven and Earth.

2

The main subject of *Principia Ethica* is 'good', and how it is to be defined.

'This question, how "good" is to be defined,' Moore wrote, 'is the most fundamental question in all Ethics'; and 'Unless this first question be fully understood, and its true answer clearly recognized, the rest of Ethics is as good as useless from the point of view of systematic knowledge.'[2]

Thus a value-concept, not Duty, is treated as the primary ethical concept, and Moore justifies this procedure as follows:

> Ethical questions are commonly asked in an ambiguous form. It is asked, 'What is a man's duty under these circumstances?' or 'Is it right to act in this way?' or 'What ought we to aim at securing?' But all these questions are capable of further analysis; a correct answer to any of them involves both judgements of what is good in itself and casual judgements. This is implied even by those who maintain that we have a direct and immediate judgement of absolute rights and duties. Such a judgement *can only mean* that the course of action in question is the *best* thing to do; that by acting so, every good that *can* be secured will have been secured (p. 24. First italics mine).

Moore's arbitrary decision as to what certain typical judgements can only mean recalls Bentham's similarly arbitrary decree that 'ought' and 'right' and 'wrong' must have no meaning except when derived from the 'principle of utility'. Both these philosophers simply brush aside the very different meanings often given to these expressions by other philosophers and by laymen.

[1] *Two Memoirs*, p. 82.
[2] *Principia Ethica*, p. 6. All page numbers without further indication refer to *Principia Ethica* (C.U.P. 1922).

Like the Utilitarians Moore does not recognize any distinction between the right and ought of expediency and the Right and Ought of Duty.

3

Moore's approach to 'good' might be termed 'realist-idealist', in that he calls it an 'object or idea':

> My business is solely with that object or idea, which I hold, rightly or wrongly, that the word [good] is generally used to stand for. What I want to discover is the nature of that object or idea, and about this I am extremely anxious to arrive at an agreement (p. 6).

This sentence itself already shows that Moore was indeed *wrong* in his notion of what the word good is 'generally used to stand for', and that he was mistaken in supposing that he was going to treat of it. For the use of 'good' to stand for an *object* is most unusual, seeing that this word—as Moore himself observes shortly afterwards—is an adjective. That it generally stands for an idea, however, may be admitted.

Just how remote Moore's 'good' is from the 'good' of basic evaluation may be judged from the following:

> Our first conclusion as to the subject-matter of Ethics is, then, that there is a simple, indefinable, unanalysable object of thought . . . By what name we call this unique object is a matter of indifference, so long as we clearly recognize what it is and that it does differ from other objects (p. 21).

(The object in question is 'good'.) But very soon it transpires that the answer to 'the most fundamental question in all Ethics' is dusty indeed, for

> If I am asked, 'What is good?' my answer is that good is good, and that is the end of the matter. Or if I am asked, 'How is good to be defined?' my answer is that it cannot be defined, and that is all I have to say about it (p. 7).

This is because,

> . . . 'good' is a simple notion, just as 'yellow' is a simple notion; [and] just as you cannot, by any manner of means, explain to anyone who does not already know it, what yellow is, so you cannot explain what good is (p. 7).

Good as an object (or idea) which can be thought of in isolation, is then contrasted with other isolated objects (or ideas) such as horses, in order to show that unlike them, it is not composite, and so 'cannot be defined':

> You can give a definition of a horse, because a horse has many different properties and qualities, all of which you can enumerate. But when you have enumerated them all, when you have reduced a horse to his simplest terms, then you can no longer define those terms (p. 8).

(This comparison hardly supports the claim of 'good' to be an object; for the 'properties and qualities' of a horse can surely not be held to include objects like his tail, which are as 'definable' in Moore's sense as the horse himself. And his properties and qualities such as swiftness or tameness are not *components* of the horse at all.)

Having thus established the indefinability of 'good' as an object or idea, and also of 'good' as an adjective, Moore turns his attention to yet another 'good', which is distinguished as '*The* good, that which is good', which is 'the substantive to which the adjective "good" will apply'. That this latter concept is central to the whole purpose of *Principia Ethica* is emphasized:

> I do not mean to say that *the* good, that which is good, is thus indefinable; if I did think so I should not be writing on Ethics, for my main object is to help towards discovering that definition (pp. 8–9).

The nature of '*the* good, that which is good' is explained as follows:

> [It] must be the whole of that to which the adjective will apply, and the adjective must *always* truly apply to it. But if it is that to which the adjective will apply it must be something different from that adjective itself, and the whole of that something different, whatever it is, will be our definition of *the* good (p. 9).

The assertion that 'good' is an adjective, and that it is different from the substantive to which it 'will apply' may seem to amount to hardly more than the statement that the adjective 'good' is an adjective and nothing but an adjective. Yet this seemingly sterile observation has given birth to a *new* object (or idea) which is presented to us as entirely distinct from that one for which the solitary word 'good' stands; this new object or idea being *the* good.

This seems to have come about through the ambiguous use of the word 'substantive', which is here made to stand not only for a grammatical term but also for a 'something', the shift of sense being also helped by the expression 'will apply', not 'applies', which would have tied down the exposition to the subject of grammatical usage with which it started. So now we have a something which is *the* good, and this something is distinguished by the fact that the adjective 'good' must apply to the whole of it, and further, must *always* truly apply to it. It would seem to follow from this that if anything existed to the whole of which the adjective 'good' would apply, and to the whole of which it would *always* truly apply we should be entitled to call it *the* good, but not otherwise.

From the italicized *the* and the singular 'that'—'that which is good' and not 'those things which are good', or similarly—as well as the reference to 'that something different', the reader now naturally expects a definition of some *one* thing 'which is good'—Happiness, possibly, or Beauty?—forgetting perhaps that since GOOD[1] is an *object*, GOOD itself would in this case have to be accorded the unique distinction of being '*the* good' —and that would be 'the end of the matter'. A sobering thought. Fortunately though, it transpires later than *the* good is, after all, multiple: '. . . we certainly do know a great many things that are good-in-themselves, and good in a high degree' (p. 184), and, 'Things intrinsically good and valuable are many and various' (p. 223).

> The good object [Moore proceeds] may have other adjectives besides 'good' that will apply to it; it may be full of pleasure, for example, it may be intelligent; *and if these adjectives really do apply to it, then it will certainly be true, that pleasure and intelligence are good* (p. 9. My italics).

The implications of this are sensational. On the most obvious interpretation it means that any attribute—e.g. pleasantness or intelligence—of any of the large number of good things that there are, is itself *ipso facto* good; so that if the good thing in

---

[1] For convenience I write GOOD thus in capitals to designate Moore's indefinable 'object or idea', so as to distinguish it from the adjectival 'good'.

question is, say, yellow, then 'it will certainly be true' that yellowness is good. Nay more, if the good thing is abstract, then abstractness will be good, and if it is concrete concreteness, by the same token, will be good. But this is only the beginning of the story. For if to be a good thing (i.e. to be a thing to which the adjective 'good' will apply) 'must' be to be a thing to the *whole* of which the adjective 'good' will *always* truly apply, it follows that if the original good thing is, let us say, abstract, thus conferring goodness on abstractness so that abstractness is in its turn—according to the condition laid down—wholly and always truly good, then everything which has the property of abstractness is in *its* turn wholly and always truly good: including, to take one example, evil. And by the same ruling, if the good object merely *exists*, thus conferring (total and eternal) goodness on existence, everything which has the resultantly wholly-and-always-truly-good attribute of existence[1] is wholly and always truly good . . .

I mention all this, of course, only to show what sort of misunderstandings may arise through taking Moore's axioms too literally. It soon transpires that 'that which is good', or 'the substantive to which the adjective [good] will apply' is neither a single unique wholly-and-always-good object—since as we are presently told, there are numerous things to which the adjective applies—nor yet everything in existence, despite the argument which seems to make this logically inevitable; nor yet just any one of the many things that are apt to be called good in ordinary conversation, seeing that these may be partly non-good, or may go bad if kept too long. So we must simply be content at this stage to understand that *the* good, that which is good is—or rather are—some very special things which are wholly and always good, not to be confused with things which are good or beneficial in the ordinary sense.

4

Strangely enough, in view of the importance he attaches to finding them, no things are identified by Moore as '*the* good' from beginning to end of his book. But in the final chapter two

---

[1] To forestall a possible charge of unfairness here I must mention that Moore does treat existence as an attribute (see e.g. the quotation from p. 197 in section 10 below).

'states of consciousness' are specified which, he declares, are 'worth having purely for their own sakes', and in comparison with which 'nothing else has nearly so great a value'.[1] These states of consciousness are 'the pleasures of human intercourse' and 'the enjoyment of beautiful objects' (p. 188). The special goodness of the latter is already stressed in earlier chapters, e.g.

> It seems to be true that to be conscious of a beautiful object is a thing of great intrinsic value (p. 28)

and,

> It seems to me that a pleasurable Contemplation of beauty has certainly an immeasurably greater value than mere consciousness of pleasure . . . p. 94) ;

and the fact that these and similar references to the goodness of beauty and the appreciation of it are almost the only expressions of opinion about the intrinsic goodness of anything right up to the final chapter naturally tends to prepare our minds for the conclusions there set down. But there is very little else to support them. They have been preceded, it is true, by an elaborate piece of analysis designed to show that the goodness of a *whole* is not the same as the sum of the goodness of its parts, but this is quite sterile because no criterion for determining goodness is ever proposed—naturally not, since according to Moore 'there is no criterion of goodness' (p. 138). The use of the terms 'worth' and 'value' as above—*'worth having* . . .—nothing else has nearly so great a *value* . . .'—may mean anything or nothing, since although references to value occur repeatedly throughout the book, Moore gives us no criterion of value either. If it were possible to assume that the 'basic' standard is being used as a matter of course we could take it that Moore's claim for the supreme value of his two 'goods' rests solely on his having come to the conclusion that most people do in fact prefer them to anything else; and as will be seen, the suggestion that they must do so is actually made a part of the claim. But since Moore has by then been

[1] P. 188. As a comment on the difficulty of deciding in any given case whether some word or phrase in *Principia Ethica* is being used to stand for 'good' in this sense or in that, I may cite a list compiled by A. Edel of terms which are there declared or implied to be synonymous with 'good': Intrinsic value; intrinsic worth; ought to exist; absolutely good; good in itself; ought to be. (From *The Philosophy of G. E. Moore.* Northwestern University Press.) To this list may be added 'worth having for its own sake'.

at particular pains to give reasons for rejecting the Utilitarians' criterion of value, according to which the value of anything is determined by human preferences, without replacing it by anything else, his 'value', like his GOOD and his good, remains veiled in mystery.

5

Moore's famous attack on Hedonism is often said to have been an important contribution to ethical theory because it disposed once and for all of the hedonistic fallacy of supposing that 'nothing is good but pleasure' (p. 59). The remarkable fact is, however, that neither Sidgwick nor Mill, who were singled out for criticism on this head, ever did make this claim for pleasure, and that throughout the whole course of his polemic Moore did not produce one quotation (though he quoted heavily, especially from Mill) which even remotely suggests that they did.

The chapter entitled Hedonism begins as follows:

> In this chapter we have to deal with what is perhaps the most famous and the most widely held of all ethical principles—the principle that nothing is good but pleasure (p. 59).

This is shortly afterwards referred to as 'the precise definition [of hedonism] used above' (p. 61). Two paragraphs later, however, the position of the hedonists is stated thus:

> All other things but pleasure, whether conduct or virtue or knowledge, whether life or nature or beauty, *are* only *good* as a means to pleasure, or for the sake of pleasure; never for their own sakes or as ends in themselves (p. 63, My italics).

So already we find Moore contradicting his previous assertion that the hedonists uphold the principle that 'nothing is good but pleasure' and supplying a generous list of the other things which, according to him, they might *also* assert to be good. On this piece of muddled misrepresentation Moore bases a cardinal point in his 'refutation' of hedonism, as we shall see.

Not unnaturally, neither Mill nor Sidgwick nor, probably, any other reputable hedonist philosopher has ever attempted to maintain that nothing is entitled to be called good except pleasure. On the contrary, as most of us know, the typical hedonist *starts* from the observation that various things are good and goes on to claim that these things are good in

proportion as they promote pleasure—or happiness—which they
call the only *ultimate* good. Both Sidgwick and Mill are careful
in distinguishing between 'good as means' and 'good as end'
or 'intrinsically good', just as Moore himself is:

> We commonly say 'such and such a thing is good'. But in the
> one case 'good' will mean 'good as means', i.e., merely that
> the thing is a means to good—will have good effects; in the
> other case it will mean 'good as end'—we shall be judging that
> the thing itself has the property which, in the first case, we
> only asserted to belong to its effects (p. 24),

only Moore hedges in a way that they do not, by trying to
make out that 'in the one case' when we say 'such and such a
thing is good' we are not *really* saying that *it* is good. Mill
states his position as follows in a passage (from Chapter IV of
his *Utilitarianism*) actually quoted by Moore at the beginning
of his attack:

> The Utilitarian doctrine is that happiness [previously defined
> as 'pleasure and the absence of pain'] is desirable, and the only
> thing desirable, as an end; all other things being only desirable
> as means to that end.

(He does not say in so many words that 'desirable' is a synonym
here for 'good' but we may take it, with Moore, that he does
mean this.)

One might have expected that Moore, having noticed the
distinction drawn by Mill between means and ends would have
confined his criticism to the proposition that 'pleasure is the
only thing good (or desirable) *as an end*.' But no. 'Mill,' he says,
'admits that other things than pleasure are desired, and this
admission is at once a contradiction of his Hedonism'. 'What,'
Moore demands magisterially, 'is the doctrine which is at all
events essential to Mill's argument?' And answers himself, 'It
is this. That when I desire the wine it is not the wine which I
desire but the pleasure which I expect to get from it' (p.70).
Mill's alleged inconsistency in holding that nothing is good
except pleasure and also that things which *give* pleasure are
good as well is harped upon through page after page: 'He has
to prove that we always do desire pleasure or freedom from
pain, and that we never desire anything else whatever' (p. 73);
and, 'He insists that we do *actually* desire other things than
pleasure, and yet he says we do *really* desire nothing else' (p. 74).

At the end of the chapter on hedonism, and even now and then in the course of it, hedonism is called the doctrine that pleasure is the only thing which is good *in itself*, and this tacit acknowledgement that Mill has only claimed a special *kind* of exclusive goodness for pleasure makes the contempt which Moore heaps on his own version 'nothing is good but pleasure', all the more surprising.

On reflection one must suspect that this extraordinary muddle is somehow connected with Moore's own conception of good as an *object*. Early on he treats of 'the naturalistic fallacy', of which he says the hedonists are guilty; and the propositions of the hedonists that he cites as characteristic of the naturalistic fallacy are that 'good is pleasure' and that 'good is that which is desired' (p. 11). But *these are not quotations*. Moore made them up himself, and though presented as if they formed the essential basis of every hedonist philosophy, they are no more than what he supposed, and apparently wished, the hedonists to assert; and what he did was to arbitrarily-translate their statement that pleasure is good into 'good is pleasure', much as if we were to translate 'daffodils are yellow' into 'yellow is daffodils'. 'Good', as Moore himself has reminded us, is an adjective; and if he had kept this in mind, and had also noticed that 'alone good as an end' is an adjectival phrase, he would have had to look for other grounds on which to accuse the hedonists of saying not only that pleasure is the only thing which is good, but also of saying in effect that pleasure is identical with his own 'indefinable object' GOOD. But he would have looked in vain.

As to 'good is that which is desired': this seems to be derived —still by the method of turning other people's adjectives into nouns—from Mill's assertion that 'to think of an object as desirable (unless for the sake of its consequences) and to think of it as pleasant, are one and the same'. By treating 'pleasant' as synonymous with 'good', and then with his own GOOD, Moore got the same kind of result as before.

6

Another of Mill's errors, according to Moore, was to hold that whilst nothing but pleasure is good, some kinds of pleasure are

superior in quality to others. Moore is extremely derisive about
this, but hardly with justice, since his version of what Mill
meant by qualitative superiority omits the main point in
Mill's *own* account of what he meant by it, in the relevant
passage which Moore himself again quotes:

> If I am asked what I mean by difference of quality in pleasures,
> or what makes one pleasure more valuable than another,
> merely as a pleasure, except its being greater in amount, there
> is but one possible answer. Of two pleasures, if there be one
> to which all or almost all who have experience of both give a
> decided preference, irrespective of any feeling of moral obliga-
> tion to prefer it, that is the more desirable pleasure. If one of
> the two is, by those who are competently acquainted with
> both, placed so far above the other *that they prefer it, even though
> knowing it to be attended with a greater amount of discontent,* and
> would not resign it for any quantity of the other pleasure which
> their nature is capable of, we are justified in ascribing to the
> preferred enjoyment a superiority in quality, so far outweighing
> quantity as to render it, in comparison, of small account
> (*Utilitarianism*, Chapter II).

Moore, ignoring the passage I have italicized, comments as
follows:

> It will be seen that Mill's test for one pleasure's superiority in
> quality over another is the preference of most people who have
> experienced both . . . But then, as we have seen, he holds that
> 'to think of an object as desirable and to think of it as pleasant
> are one and the same thing' . . . he holds, therefore, that the
> preference of experts merely proves that one pleasure is
> pleasanter than another' (p. 78).

Mill's test for the qualitative superiority of a pleasure—the
extent of the sacrifice one is prepared to make in order to enjoy
it—seems to anticipate the criterion of the Viennese 'psychological' school of economists for assessing relative value: an
interesting theory, surely, and worthy of consideration. Moore,
however, prefers to pass over Mill's test—apart from including
it in his quotation—and then to represent Mill as having been
unable to find any support for his concept of qualitative
superiority except quantity.

It is interesting to notice, in this connection, that Moore's
own claim of qualitative superiority for certain pleasurable ex-

periences—the pleasures of human intercourse and the enjoyment of beautiful objects—is supported, not by any argument, but by an appeal to what 'any one will think'.[1] Anyone, presumably, who is acquainted with the experiences: or, as Moore would say, any 'expert'.

It may be remarked that if Mill had not given a criterion of superiority for pleasures, but had been content to say only that some pleasures are *intrinsically* superior to others, Moore, of all people, would have been the least entitled to object. For anyone who, like Mill and Moore, but unlike the present writer, admits the notion of intrinsic superiority, and who also believes that pleasure can take various forms, there is no logical objection to holding that some forms of it are intrinsically superior—so long, of course, as he does not try to prove it, or to define intrinsic superiority. Intrinsic value is purely a matter of intuition anyhow; so if we have an inner conviction that the pleasure of reading Pushkin is superior to the pleasure of playing pushpin there seems no reason for not saying so, and nobody can contradict us.

7

Another of Mills 'mistakes', to which Moore devotes particular attention, consists in his alleged failure to notice that he must necessarily be wrong in holding that pleasure *alone*, i.e. pleasure unaccompanied by anything else whatever, would be any good at all. 'Can it really be said,' Moore demands, 'that we value pleasure except in so far as we are conscious of it? Should we think that the attainment of pleasure, of which we never were and never could be conscious, was something to be aimed at for its own sake?' (p. 87). And much more to the same effect. Moore seems to have been indebted to Plato for this argument, and he quotes the following exchange between Socrates and Protarchus in support of it:

> *Socrates:* Would *you* accept, Protarchus . . . to live your whole life in the enjoyment of the greatest pleasures?
> *Protarchus:* Of course I would.

[1] '. . . nor . . . does it appear probable that any one will think that anything else has *nearly* so great a value . . .' (pp. 88–89. The full passage will be quoted in section 10.)

Socrates : Then would you think you needed anything else
besides, if you possessed this one blessing in completeness?
Protarchus : Certainly not.
Socrates : Consider what you are saying. You would not need to
be wise and intelligent and reasonable, nor anything like this?
Protarchus : Why should I? I suppose I should have all I want
if I were pleased.

After this, of course, Socrates has it all his own way. But
Protarchus, if he had not been a fool—or rather if he had not
been what comedians call a stooge—would never have allowed
himself to be trapped in the position of trying to argue that
pleasure is something which can exist without the presence of
either intelligence or senses. Protarchus should have replied
somewhat as follows: 'Naturally I should need to be wise, and
intelligent, and reasonable in order to live my whole life in
the enjoyment of the greatest pleasures. For among my very
greatest pleasures is the privilege of discourse with you, Socrates,
to which end I find the possession of my highest mental faculties
indispensable.'

Moore's criticism of Mill and Sidgwick on this score derived
its whole force from the presumption that by 'pleasure' they
mean some isolated 'object' which exists irrespective of whether
anyone is experiencing it : much like Moore's own indefinable
GOOD. But of course it is quite clear, and clear even from
extracts from their writings which Moore quotes, that they
never meant anything of the sort. In common with most of us
they regarded pleasure as a feeling, and it does not seem even
to have occurred to them to explain, in anticipation of Moore's
line of criticism, that it cannot exist without anyone's having it.

Afterwards, with a show of magnanimity, Moore admits that
perhaps what Mill is really talking about is 'consciousness of
pleasure', and not pleasure all by itself. But this, he says, will
not do either :

> The method which I employed in order to shew that pleasure
> itself was not the sole good was that of considering what value
> we should attach to it if it existed in absolute isolation. [This
> method] seems also to shew that consciousness of pleasure is
> itself far less valuable than other things (p. 91).

The enjoyment of beautiful objects, for example.

It may be conceded that Mill's anxiety to reconcile his hedonism with his awareness that things are apt to be desired for their own sakes rather than consciously for the sake of pleasure or happiness leads him to make use of some doubtful expressions. Money, he remarks, is sometimes desired for its own sake instead of for the happiness it may be expected to purchase. But in this case, he says, it is still being desired as 'a part of happiness.' This is hardly worse than a clumsy metaphor but Moore pounces on it with acrimony:

> Does Mill really mean to say that 'money', these actual coins which he admits to be desired in and for themselves, are a part either of pleasure or of the absence of pain? Will he maintain that these coins themselves are in my mind, and actually a part of my pleasant feeling? (p. 71).

The obvious answer is that of course Mill doesn't, and of course he won't; but Moore goes on ... 'This contemptible nonsense,' he says, and actually (p. 72) proceeds to invent a piece of dialogue between himself and Mill in which Mill feebly tries to defend his 'parts of happiness', his last remark being, 'I dare say the public won't notice.'

Such were the methods Moore employed in sweeping from his path everything which he saw as a possible obstacle to his own conclusions.

8

In contrast to his treatment of the hedonists, Moore lets off the metaphysicians very lightly. The content of the chapter headed Metaphysical Ethics has little relevance to the present study, and it may be remarked that if Moore had really only been concerned to deal in his book with what the word good 'is generally used to stand for', instead of with GOOD as an object, it would have had as little relevance to *Principia Ethica*, except as illustrating two irreconcilably different lines of approach to the subject of evaluation. The ethical metaphysicians—among whom Moore himself must be numbered by virtue of his definition of GOOD as a unique, indefinable object—make statements about Nature, or Reality, on the one hand, and GOOD, or The Ideal, on the other, and try to establish various logical relations between them; or as in Moore's case, to show that no such relations can be established.

The other, non-metaphysical, approach is to inquire into what value terms are generally used to stand for.

Moore has no difficulty in showing that Metaphysics as 'the investigation of a supposed supersensible reality' can have 'no logical bearing whatever' upon the answer to 'the fundamental ethical question "What is good in itself?"' And he points out that this follows in any case' from the conclusion of Chapter I that "good" denotes an ultimate, unanalysable predicate' (p. 140).

9

Before coming to his supreme 'goods' Moore devotes a chapter to the subject of *Ethics in Relation to Conduct*, in which he repeats his assertion (see section 2 above) that the significance of ethical judgements is derived from the idea of 'good', and declares it to be 'demonstrably certain' that the assertion 'I am morally bound to perform this action' is identical with the assertion 'This action will produce the greatest possible amount of good in the universe'. His demonstration runs as follows:

> It is plain that when we assert that a certain action is our absolute duty, we are asserting that the performance of that action at that time is unique in respect of value. But no dutiful action can possibly have unique value in the sense that it is the sole thing of value in the world; since, in that case, *every* such act would be the *sole* good thing, which is a manifest contradiction. And for the same reason its value cannot be unique in the sense that it has more intrinsic value than anything else in the world; since *every* act of duty would then be the *best* thing in the world, which is also a contradiction. It can, therefore, be unique only in the sense that the whole world will be better, if it be performed, than if any possible alternative were taken (p. 147).

The phrase 'unique in respect of value' is interesting as suggesting that very distinction between ethical and non-ethical evaluation which, I have argued, it is necessary to draw in order to escape from the moralistic entanglement of basic evaluation with the evaluation derived from the unique ethical concept of Duty—Kant's use of 'good' in his Good Will is the classic example of the latter. But in the context of Moore's Moralism—his failure to draw any distinction between ethical and non-ethical value judgements—his 'unique in respect of value' is incomprehensible, and the argument here based on it equally so. The more straightforward and lucid formulation in Chapter I which is supposed to produce the same conclusion plainly makes use of basic evaluation:

> In short, to assert that a certain line of conduct is, at a given time, absolutely right or obligatory, is obviously to assert that more good and less evil will exist in the world if it be adopted than if anything else be done instead (p. 25).

But, leaving aside the question of criteria, what Moore declares to be obvious is surely very far from being so. On the lips of a devout Christian the statement that some line of conduct is absolutely right or obligatory would be much more likely to mean that it would be pleasing to God; and on the lips of a Kantian moralist it would mean either that it is conduct which the person's 'moral will' enjoins upon him, or else that it conforms to a principle which he regards as universally obligatory, regardless of what its effects may be. Moore's idea of what is to be understood by 'right' or 'obligatory' resembles the Utilitarians', at least with respect to its main consequence: that the morality of an act is not determined by the motive for performing it, but by its results. (On this principle it would seem that even an involuntary act such as having a fit in the Reading Room of the British Museum might, as promoting the pleasures of human intercourse, be absolutely right and obligatory, according to Moore.) The objection to this criterion of morality from the point of view of the Ethicist is that it leaves no room for the concept of Duty, or the sense of Duty, or the Ought, as determinant of the moral act. The objection from the point of view of the reader who wants to understand Moore's *principia ethica* is that it leaves no room for a principle according to which it *is* right or obligatory to maximize the good.

However, a corollary, acceptable to Moore, of the view that the morality of an act is to be judged by its results is that the moral value of actions can only be judged retrospectively, and this he stresses. If the action promoted the good it was moral. If not, not. And seeing that the whole consequences of an action can never be known, Moore concludes that there is little reason to depart from conformity to existing laws and customs, and indeed that we Ought not to depart from them. It seems doubtful, he says:

> ... whether Ethics can establish the utility of any rules other than those generally practised. But its inability to do so is fortunately of little practical moment. The question whether the general observance of a rule not generally observed, would or would not be desirable, cannot much affect the question how any individual ought to act, since, on the one hand, there is a large possibility that he will not, by any means, be able to bring about its general observance, and, on the other hand, the fact that its general observance would be useful could, in any case, give him no reason to conclude that he himself ought to observe it in the absence of any such general observance ... In short, though we may be sure that there are cases where the rule should be broken, we can never know which those cases are, and ought, therefore, never to break it (pp. 161–3).

This not very resounding maxim has the distinction of being the only specific moral precept anywhere in the book. We ought never to break the existing rules because we are unlikely to be able to change them, and because we can never *know* when it is Right to break them. Thus we are offered no guidance on how to act under the threat of new rules which would inhibit the pleasures of free human intercourse or—perhaps in the cause of 'social realism'—the enjoyment of what we regard as beautiful objects; but it seems plain at least that once the rules are established we Ought to adhere to them. With respect to conduct, apparently, 'that which is good' is Conformity.

10

Having dealt with the hedonists and the metaphysicians, Moore proceeds to his exposition of '*the* good', or, as he expresses it on p. 187, 'what things are such that if they existed *by themselves*, in absolute isolation, we should yet judge their existence to be good.' The two things of this kind which he identifies are, as we know, two 'states of consciousness' of two sorts of pleasure, although their goodness, we are presumably to understand, does not inhere in their pleasantness; since to believe this would be to fall into the error of Hedonism.

It is not even claimed that anything in the impressive argumentative structure built up beforehand has actually yielded the two great 'goods' which appear in the final chapter. It is admitted at the beginning of this chapter that 'to the fundamental question of Ethics—the question "What things are goods or ends in themselves?" . . . we have hitherto obtained only a negative answer: the answer that pleasure is certainly not the *sole* good' (p. 184). Since Moore, as we have seen, had been quite unable to show that anybody ever said it was, this is certainly a modest claim enough, and we are now invited to accept the two great goods, rather surprisingly, by a straightforward appeal to public opinion as follows:

> By far the most valuable things which we know or can imagine, are certain states of consciousness, which may be roughly described as the pleasures of human intercourse and the enjoyment of beautiful objects. No one, probably, who has asked himself the question, has ever doubted that personal affection and the appreciation of what is beautiful in Art or Nature, are good in themselves; nor, if we consider strictly what things are worth having *purely for their own sakes*, does it appear probable that any one will think that anything else has *nearly* so great a value as the things which are included under these two heads.

And,

> It is, I think, universally admitted that the proper appreciation of a beautiful object is a good thing in itself . . . (pp. 188–9).

As it happens, there is one rather serious objection to these conclusions; an objection which relates to Moore's own test for goodness and value. This is what I think may be called the 'isolation test'. It will be remembered that in that part of his criticism of the hedonists in which he represented their doctrine fairly as 'pleasure alone is good as an end' Moore tried to demonstrate its obvious falsity by inquiring whether pleasure 'in absolute isolation' could be a good thing at all; and concluded that it would in any case not be very good because consciousness would also be requisite in order that the pleasure should be had (see section 7 above). But 'consciousness of pleasure' in its turn was then subjected to the isolation test, and also failed to pass. Here Moore was emphatic:

> Could we accept, as a very good thing, that mere consciousness of pleasure, and absolutely nothing else, should exist, even in the greatest quantities? I think we can have no doubt about answering: No (p. 94).

Now what is sauce for the goose is sauce for the gander, more especially if the gander has prepared the sauce himself; and we are surely entitled to ask on the model of the above, Could we accept, as a very good thing, that the mere state of consciousness of the pleasure of human intercourse, or the mere state of consciousness of the enjoyment of beautiful objects, and absolutely nothing else, should exist, even in the greatest quantities? I think we can have no doubt about answering: No. For would a state of consciousness of enjoying beautiful objects be a very good thing in absolute isolation—without any beautiful objects to enjoy? This is a perfectly fair question in Moore's terms, for if he had objected that the phrase 'the enjoyment of beautiful objects' presupposes the presence of beautiful objects to be enjoyed we should have pointed out that a beautiful object is no part of a 'state of consciousness' 'in absolute isolation'. The same goes for the pleasures of human intercourse, since people are required for this.

However, I do not want to labour the point, for it is sufficiently obvious that the isolation test is completely worthless and impossible, no matter what was the purpose for which it was devised. But it is certainly a little surprising to find how completely the author of the test forgot it himself when he went on to elaborate his plea for recognition of his two 'goods'. There are many instances of this forgetfulness, but it will be enough to cite a single example. On p. 197 the following occurs:

> We can imagine the case of a single person, enjoying throughout eternity the contemplation of scenery as beautiful, and intercourse with persons as admirable, as can be imagined; while yet the whole of the objects of his cognition are absolutely unreal. I think we should definitely pronounce the existence of a universe, which consisted solely of such a person, to be *greatly* inferior in value to one in which the objects, in the existence of which he believes, did really exist, just as he believes them to do.

This shows the enjoyment of beautiful objects which are actual, and the pleasures of intercourse with real admirable persons being treated as superior to the isolated 'states of consciousness' called 'the pleasures of human intercourse' and 'the enjoyment of beautiful objects'. These states of consciousness are not, then, after all, so much worth having *purely for their own sakes* as in combination with other things which they do not include: which are actual, and so extrinsic to the states of consciousness which have yet been said to be of supreme value in isolation. So much for the isolation test as applied to Moore's own specified 'goods'.

As to the persuasively-phrased appeal to public opinion: Moore was of course perfectly entitled to make it, but the assumption that everybody who reflected on the question of what is valuable must agree with his tastes was really very naïve. It is notorious that many people prefer the pleasures of the table, or of literature, or of the company of animals, to those of human intercourse; and even an aesthete might be expected to know that many of those who are capable of greatly enjoying the contemplation of beautiful objects regard this employment as a waste of time if indulged in to excess, and that there are others, even, who much prefer the arduous joys of creating objects, whether beautiful or not, to any amount of passive contemplation. Tastes differ, which may be just as well.

11

To round off this brief study of Moore's famous book we may note that certain practical conclusions would actually follow from his analysis, supposing his unsupported premises were acceptable; conclusions which, strangely enough, are nowhere set down by Moore himself.

If it were the case that everyone is really agreed in holding that the pleasures of human intercourse and the enjoyment of beautiful objects are supremely good, and if it were also the case that anyone who says some action is absolutely right and obligatory means that to do it will increase the amount of good in the world (see section 9 above), it would certainly follow that all who speak in these terms must agree that it is absolutely

right and obligatory to promote the pleasures of human intercourse, etc., so that they could say, 'It is our Duty to promote
the pleasures, etc.', and this would be a true universal ethical
imperative. It would, however, have to be qualified in Moore's
system by the condition that we ought never to break an established rule; so that the imperative would run, 'It is our Duty
to promote the pleasures, etc., when this does not involve
breaking an established rule.'

It is, I believe, impossible to place the above conclusions in
any logical relation to Moore's much-stressed dictum that
'pleasure is not the sole good'; the positive opposite of which,
incidentally, only Aunt Sally Protarchus seems ever to have
upheld.

12

Principia Ethica has both followed, and helped to direct, the
change of emphasis in moral philosophy from the practical to
the analytical. It was first welcomed as an inspiring call to
embrace an attitude to life which deserved, though it did not
claim, the title of The Higher Hedonism. It was a Hedonism
which made Utilitarianism seem by contrast commonplace and
crude. But not only was the message inspiring, it was supported
by all the authority of an impressive analysis of the concept
'good'. This analysis did not really provide any logical backing
for the evaluative conclusions reached at the end, but its effect
was to make them appear as a superior alternative to the
Utilitarians'—equally baseless, but, some may feel, wiser and
nicer—conclusion that it is our Duty to promote the greatest
happiness of the greatest number.

Moore's book is certainly a curiosity, and it has played an
important role in moral philosophy through its interfusing of
Ethics with axiology. I judge it to be a bad book in more ways
than one. It has plunged the concept of goodness to new depths
of obscurity and confusion, making it more difficult than ever
to separate ethical from non-ethical evaluation; and it has done
this in a period when for many reasons it has seemed especially
important for us to think directly and clearly about values in
relation to human aims.

8

THE LANGUAGE OF MORALS

The chief end of language in communication being to be understood, words serve not well for that end, neither in civil nor philosophical discourse, when any word does not excite in the hearer the same idea which it stands for in the mind of the speaker.

JOHN LOCKE

SUMMARY: Hume pointed out that to derive ethical imperatives from factual statements is a logical impossibility. Whilst few moral philosophers nowadays are prepared to challenge this conclusion, attempts are still made to take the sting out of it by arguing that *value statements* carry with them an *implicit* ethical imperative. R. M. Hare is a distinguished exponent of this view. Though differentiating between ethical and non-ethical value statements he contends that both are a form of *command*. In arguing to this effect he ends by reducing the status of the value statement to the level of a mere expression of approval or disapproval combined with the implied desire that certain acts should be performed or certain lines of action followed. I criticize these conclusions, which contradict my claim for the impersonality and informativeness of basic-value statements, and their debatability and testability as propositions.

I

The moral philosophies of Kant, Bentham, and Moore are in the sharpest contrast, but, as I have tried to show, they are all marked by logical faults which could have been avoided by sticking to Kant's rigorous demarcation between common values and ethical Values.

Kant tried to divorce his ethical Good altogether from the

L

idea of beneficence, and he held to his purpose so far that his Good Will does not, and as moral *must* not, have good intentions: must not aim at benefiting either its possessor or anyone else. This simply followed from the condition that the Good Will has *no other aim* than to obey the sense of Duty. But Kant was not content to let this condition speak for itself: he was explicit in making the point that the desire to do good (he took no account of the desire that good should *be done*) is not Good—is not, i.e., moral. (See Chapter 5, section 3 above.) However, as we saw, Kant could not, after all, help bringing to the service of his ethic the idea of what is good-as-beneficent, because as well as defining his Good Will he wanted to *recommend* it. Therefore he was obliged to argue firstly that the Good will was also good, in that it would purge its owner of arrogance and other forms of disagreeableness, and secondly that the principles which, so he held, the Good Will must embrace— veracity in particular—would conduce both to its owner's advantage and to the advantage of society at large. Even so, Kant, for all his backslidings, did succeed in defining the purely and distinctively moral act by identifying it as the act performed *from* Duty, and nothing but Duty. This is perhaps the most revolutionary single contribution to ethical theory ever made, and it is no doubt chiefly because moral philosophers have always recognized the unique achievement of Kant in defining and circumscribing the idea of the *purely* moral or ethical that he is still widely regarded as the greatest [moral philosopher of them all. At the same time, however, Kant's lapses into Moralism, his betrayal of his own achievement by corrupting his 'Duty' with consideration of expediency and his Good with goodness have probably produced worse chaos in certain departments of ethical theory than any other philosopher has wrought before or since.

2

Whilst Kant made Good in relation to motive and conduct a *purely ethical* concept by linking it to Duty, Bentham tried to link Duty to goodness, and failed, as we saw. Just as Kant when he came to elaborate his thesis, could not bring himself to dispense with the common idea of goodness, so Bentham in elaborating his counsels of expediency could not resist the temptation to invoke the support of Duty. Even as Kant was beguiled into inconsistency by the wish to make his principles just a little attractive, so Bentham, because he wanted to advance every available sort of inducement towards adopting his, was led to seek the blessing of moral Duty, to the confounding of Utilitarianism as a consistent theory of conduct.

3

Moore's theory is peculiar in every sense of the word; but his tangled sophistries, the result of trying to force a way out of the ethical impasse created by the Utilitarians, are important as showing the low level to which non-Kantian Ethics had then sunk. Heavily influenced by the absolutism of Plato, Moore with his GOOD introduced a concept—if that is the word for it— which bore little relation either to the ethical Duty-Good or to the good of benefit. His '*the* good, that which is good' is presented so confusingly that it is impossible to tell what it is supposed to embrace, and his conclusions as to the particular things which are particularly good emerge purely as expressions of his personal tastes. His attempts to relate goodness to Duty failed conspicuously, for he could find nothing to justify his assertion that to say that a certain line of conduct is Right is 'obviously' to say that it will increase the amount of good in the world.

4

Hume's famous comment on the impossibility of deriving a moral imperative from a factual statement[1] was, and still is, a tremendous stimulus to moral philosophizing. All Hume really did was to draw the Ethicists' attention to the simple rule of

[1] In every system of morality which I have hitherto met with I have always remarked that the author proceeds for some time in the ordinary way of reasoning, and establishes the being of a God, or makes observations concerning human affairs; when of a sudden I am surprised to find, that instead of the usual copulations of propositions, *is*, and *is not*, I meet with no proposition that is not connected with an *ought*, or an *ought not*. This change is imperceptible; but it is, however, of the last consequence. For as this *ought* or *ought not* expresses some new relation or affirmation, it is necessary that it should be observed and explained; and at the same time that a reason should be given for what seems altogether inconceivable, how this new relation can be a deduction from others that are entirely different from it. (*Treatise*, Book III, 1, section i.)

logic according to which no term can occur in the conclusion
of a syllogism which was not in one of the premises. He would
have found no fault with such a formula as 'What God commands is what Ought to be done: God commands *a*, therefore
a Ought to be done'. And he would have regarded as equally
beyond reproach the formula 'What M ought to do is what
furthers the end he has in view: *a* furthers the end M has in
view, therefore *a* is what M ought to do', which conforms to
our non-ethical usage of 'ought' as applied to conduct. This is
the ought used in advice and also in expressions of opinion
which are not necessarily advisory—'Obviously he ought not
to do that if he wants so-and-so'—and like the non-ethical
'right' and 'wrong' (see Chapter 6, section 5 above) it has
nothing to do with the ought-criterion of ethical judgements,
according to which 'he ought to . . .' means 'it is his Duty
to . . .' Nevertheless it seems to be felt by very many moral
philosophers that Hume's comment is a challenge that must
be met—or at least an obstruction that must be removed, in
order that the unpremised moral Ought may be logically
justified in some way or other after all. This attitude is no doubt
partly due to misgivings lest our behaviour should become even
more depraved than it is now, if we were to notice that the
moral Ought can have no universally valid 'because' to support
it. But it is also sustained by that spirit of intellectual tenacity
which inspired those mathematicians who devoted their
lives to the enterprise of squaring the circle, before it became
necessary to acknowledge that this was impossible. As regards
the attempt to square Hume the experts are still in good heart.

Nowadays it is usual to draw a distinction between moralists
and moral philosophers as between those who have a prescriptive axe to grind and those whose business is with the *theory*
of morals; but in fact the distinction is somewhat unreal.
Nearly all moralists, if they are not mere ranters, support their
exhortations by arguments, however unsound; and nearly all
moral philosophers, if they are not mere language-analysts,
adumbrate recommendations about conduct, or even state
them outright at the end of the book. In so far as any distinction
of this sort can be usefully drawn it is between those, on the
one hand, who begin by assuming the 'truth' of one or more
moral maxims and go on to support them by arguments from

intuition, or authority, or expediency, or all three, and those, on the other hand, whose procedure is to analyse value terminology with a view to reconciling it with moral judgements in a way which does not violate logic. Most of the moral theories which deserve to be seriously considered belong to the latter class.

In this type of inquiry Duty usually plays a very minor role, or is even ignored altogether, whilst the various uses of the word 'ought' receive much attention, because 'ought' is the word used in issuing moral imperatives. This approach leads to Moralism, since 'ought', unlike unqualified 'Duty', has two meanings, only one of which is properly ethical. Kant's observations on the matter should have acted as a warning here (see Chapter 6, section 4 above), but in fact Moralism now rules supreme in ethical theory, and those who approach the prevailing mixture of Ethics and axiology, so far from trying to separate out the various ingredients, are only intent on giving them another stir.

5

One of the most notable of recent attempts to integrate ordinary value statements and moral judgements is R. M. Hare's *The Language of Morals*.[1] This work is in many ways typical of much current ethical theory, and is an important contribution to the subject, in the modern convention of language-analysis; but my chief reason for choosing it for discussion here is that whereas it deals very largely with the subject of evaluation and distinguishes, as I do also, between moral and non-moral value statements, the way they are handled, and the conclusions reached, are so different from mine that to discuss it will enable me to challenge much of what I find most unacceptable in the prevailing treatment of Ethics and values.

The Language of Morals, like most post-Moorean moral theory, concentrates on the search for clues to the essential nature of moral judgements by investigating the meanings underlying our use of value terms—'good' particularly. The central aim is to find some significant connection between 'good' and

---

[1] O.U.P., 1952. The present chapter was written before the publication, in 1963, of Hare's *Freedom and Reason* (O.U.P.). But as I find in the later work no modification of the arguments which I attack here, and their endorsement in many places, I have no reason to revoke any part of my criticism—in spite of my warm respect for the spirit of Mr. Hare's conclusions.

'ought'. Unlike Moore, Mr. Hare is not content to dismiss this problem by saying that the connection is 'obvious'. Though taking it for granted that the connection does indeed exist, he sees the importance of explaining this, and he propounds an ingenious theory to account for it.

The theory—to state it in the concisest possible terms—is that, whilst a value judgement may have a certain informative content, its main importance is that it provides some form of answer to the question 'What shall I do?' For every value judgement commends, or discommends, its subject; and this means that its function is to guide action in relation to that subject. It also implicitly evaluates other things of the same class and character as the named subject (which feature provides the element of universality which, it is claimed, belongs to all value statements). Value judgements about actions have the same prescriptive character as those about other things. To call an action good is to commend it, and to commend it is to imply that one ought to do likewise in like circumstances —similarly with value judgements on people. To call a man good is to recommend us to emulate him. These last two types of judgement are distinguished as 'moral'—the term Mr. Hare uses to denote those value judgements which relate to people and their actions—with the exception of those which merely assert 'instrumental' value, as in assessments of 'the man for the job'. So, by discovering a prescriptive element in every type of value statement, Hare links commendation (or discommendation) to recommendation, and the value statement to the moral imperative. With respect to *principles* of conduct the argument follows similar lines. All choices of action, even the most trivial, are made in accordance with a principle the agent has already accepted, or is in process of accepting, as valid. In the case of moral choices the principle chosen is the one which the agent accepts as good, or morally valid, or universally right, by the light of his own judgement, which must be the final arbiter. Thus the evaluation of 'moral' objects—i.e. men and their actions—by reference to principles, is linked to the evaluation of non-'moral' objects by reference to principles, and the moral Ought emerges as a more important, more deeply-felt form of the 'ought' of ordinary choice-guidance, as contained in any non-'moral' evaluation.

Though I may have tied up Mr. Hare's conclusions a little more tightly than is warranted by his sometimes rather diffident and qualified presentation of them, I think I have given a fair outline of the main points of his very challenging exercise in moralistic apologetics, which deals, in one way or another, with most of the main traditional difficulties.

Yet to call attention to the difficulties, and find means for getting round them, is not the same as overcoming them; and, in my view, Mr Hare completely fails, as all his predecessors and successors up to now have failed, to produce an intellectually acceptable account of the alleged connection between the ordinary open value statement and the moral imperative.

6

I think it is worth while to examine Mr Hare's initial approach to his main thesis in some detail, because the subsequent course of his argument depends to a large extent on a classification made in the opening pages.

He begins by inquiring into the character and function of the overt imperative—the command. Contrasting it with the indicative statement he finds a logical parallel—a command must not be self-contradictory—and concludes that 'commands ... like statements, are essentially intended for answering questions asked by rational agents' (pp. 15–16). Just as an indicative statement is essentially intended to answer the question 'What is the case?' a command is essentially intended to answer the question 'What shall I do?' And a further point of alleged resemblance between them is that it is no more the *purpose* of a command to get the hearer to act in a certain way than it is the *purpose* of an indicative statement to get him to believe something:

> Telling someone to do something, or that something is the case, is answering the question 'What shall I do?' or 'What are the facts?' When we have answered these questions the hearer knows what to do or what the facts are—if what we have told him is right. He is not necessarily thereby *influenced* one way or the other, nor have we failed if he is not; for he may *decide*' [my italics] 'to disbelieve or disobey us, and the mere telling him does nothing—and seeks to do nothing—to prevent him doing this (p. 15).

The idea that belief, like obedience, is normally a matter for decision is really not acceptable, seeing that the faculty of belief is not normally under one's control. However Hare pursues his analogy and clinches the matter as follows: '. . . commands, however much they may differ from statements are like them in this, that they consist in telling someone something, not in seeking to influence him' (p. 15).

But this likeness depends, surely, on the linguistic accident that the verb 'to tell' stands as a synonym both for 'to inform' and 'to command'. To 'tell' a person something is indeed not to 'tell' him to believe it. But to 'tell' him to do something is—to tell him to do it.

Mr Hare seems also to have misled himself by an ambiguity in the word 'function' in this place. 'No one,' he writes, 'in seeking to explain the function of indicative sentences would say they were attempts to persuade someone that something is the case . . .' (p. 15). Now if 'function' is being used as a strictly *logical* term we may admit that nobody in his senses would introduce the idea of 'attempts to persuade' into his exposition of the function of indicative sentences. But if we speak of the function of something in the non-specialized sense which means simply what it is for, or what it does, or what it is, in Hare's phrase, 'essentially intended' to do, then I, at least, should be prepared to maintain, at least, that the function of indicative statements is to enable us to persuade each other of what is the case, which is to say no more than that their function is to convey information. And if we are speaking in the same sense of the function of the command, then that function is to produce the action commanded. (This is not, of course, to say anything about the purpose for which *in any particular case* an indicative statement or a command is uttered. An indicative statement may be used to deceive, and a command may be used with the intention of producing an act of disobedience. But with respect to *function* in the sense in which Hare is, partly, using it, such instances are irrelevant. The function of the genus screwdriver is to turn screws, and this remains its function even if you or I use our screwdriver to dig weeds out of the lawn.)

The function of the command is direct and obvious—and is the same whether or not it is expressed in human speech. The distinctive squawk uttered by a hen-pheasant with chicks when she senses danger, we translate into our language as the command 'Take cover!' We regard it as a communication because she does not normally utter it unless she has chicks to whom to address it, and as a command because when she utters it they do take cover. (The Behaviourist would call the squawk a 'reaction', or something of the sort, but this is beside the point, since he would if consistent describe human communications in the same terms; but we are not at the moment talking his language.) Human beings are not so invariably obedient as chicks and when they disobey, what can we say but that the command has failed to fulfil its function in this instance?

What other function could a command have, except that of producing action? It has, says Mr Hare, the function of answering the question 'What shall I do?' But this is not the typical context of a command; it is, rather, the typical context of a piece of advice. Those who issue commands are not in the habit of waiting to be asked for them. Even advice may be given unsought, in which case one may reasonably say, 'When I want your advice I'll ask for it'; but to reply to a command, 'When I want your commands I'll ask for them', would be an irrelevance, to say the least.

In one sense, it may be said that these objections are unjust; because it soon becomes clear that part of the author's main purpose was to dissolve the distinction between commands and advice, leaving the purely unsought, arbitrary command outside his frame of reference. However, he nowhere states that he is doing this, and the point to be noticed is that by failing to draw any such distinction, and treating advice as a type of command—that is as a type of utterance which, despite certain common features, is distinct from the indicative or informative-type statement—he begins the process of separating the *value statement*—which he claims as essentially prescriptive—from the class of informative statements. But more of that later.

<h3 style="text-align:center">7</h3>

The form of advice is fairly simple. We can conceive an advisory utterance as a kind of prediction: 'If you do so-and-so such-and-such result will follow'—but what makes such a statement distinctive as advice is the assumption of the advisee's *purpose*, to which the advice is, so to speak, geared. It provides, in fact, an answer to the question 'What shall I do *to this end*?'

That we are in the habit of answering the question, 'What shall I do?' without knowing, or inferring, what the asker wants to achieve as the result of what he does, is something which only a moral philosopher intent on proving his point could imagine for one moment. It is only in the case of commands—true 'imperatives'—that the agent's purpose is irrelevant, as Kant showed in the case of the Categorical Imperative, which is the command addressed to oneself.

Mr. Hare, however, deals very summarily with what Kant, so unfortunately, called 'hypothetical imperatives'. He treats them not as any kind of statement which can ever be tested by experience, but as prescriptive formulas; preceeded, admittedly, by 'If you want —'; but this 'want', we are to understand, does not mean the same as 'be affected by a recognizable state of the feelings known as desire' (p. 34). This is proved as follows:

> If I were the Superior of a religious order whose rule ordained the complete abnegation of all desires, I could not say to a novice, 'If you feel a desire to go to the largest grocer in Oxford go to Grimbley Hughes' for this would be contrary to the rule. But I might well say 'If you want to go to the largest grocer in Oxford go to Grimbley Hughes'. For this would simply be intended to convey a piece of information that the largest grocer is Grimbley Hughes. 'Want' is here a logical term . . . (p. 34).

And also, as demonstrated, *entirely superfluous!*

Several other instances are given of sentences explicitly or implicitly prefixed by 'If you want'. One is, 'If you want to break your springs go on driving as you are at the moment' (p. 35), the whole point of which seems to be that the speaker is being ironical; but only one type is instanced—'To stop the train pull down the chain', and 'Plug in to a supply of the voltage indicated on the label'—which, being technical instruction, can properly be called advice; and with regard to the first the comment is made that it is 'neutral on the subject of whether the chain is actually to be pulled or not; that is why "Penalty for improper use £5" has to be added' (p. 36). It is difficult to see the point of this comment until we remember that the decision has already been taken to treat even this kind of advice as a form of *command*. In the second case it is admitted that we might 'perhaps' here infer the message, 'If you want your vacuum cleaner to clean your carpet without necessitating expensive repairs' (p. 36), though this is quite obviously meant to sound absurd. In fact, if we treat technical instruction as advice we need only infer in this case 'If you want to use the cleaner'; for of course, the formula of advice does not demand that reasons should be given for its content.

There is no mention at all here of typical non-technical advice, of which examples would be, 'Those who want a peaceful holiday are advised to go to Starfish-on-Sea', which is open advice addressed to 'those whom it may concern'; or, 'As you want to impress the jury with your ignorance of the whole matter I advise you to wear your most becoming hat and say nothing about insurance', which is personal advice. In both these types—as with technical instruction—later experience can show whether or not the advice was sound; though in the case of the second example the stated aim itself might prove to be mistaken in the context of a wider aim, concerning which the advice might have been, 'Don't make a show of ignorance'.

As I argued in Chapter 3 section 9, the characteristic of advice as such is that it always relates to *some* aim, whether stated or assumed. It is because the aim is so often taken for granted without being stated that a piece of advice can often be interpreted mistakenly as a command, when inquiry would reveal the aim to which it relates. Where an aim is assumed to be universal, in the sense that anyone in the given circumstances would have it, the command-interpretation is particularly easy. Whatever Kant meant by saying that it is a Duty to preserve one's life, it is nearly always assumed that one *wants* to preserve it, and that is why in the sort of situation where someone shouts 'Jump!' or 'Don't jump yet!' he does not find it necessary to prefix this by 'If you want to preserve your life', which makes it possible to interpret his words as purely imperative.

8

Hare's next step towards linking the value statement to the moral imperative is made via a discussion of principles, and the

upshot is that all our choices of action are based on decisions
of principle—'principle' figuring here as an elastic term which
covers both those rules of conduct which for one reason or
another we may accept or reject, obey or disobey, and also
those rules or habits of consistent behaviour which we inevitably
come to adopt through our expectations of consistent behaviour
by our physical environment. In this connection the concept
of prediction —the verbalized form of expectation—is introduce in rather a novel way to assist the conclusion that everything we do is done 'on principle'.

> The kind of knowledge that we have of the future—unless we
> are clairvoyant—is based upon principles of prediction which
> we are taught, or form for ourselves. Principles of prediction are
> a kind of principle of action; for to predict is to act in a certain
> way. Thus although there is nothing logically to prevent some-
> one doing entirely without principles . . . this in fact never
> occurs (p. 59).

This, followed by,

> It is important to remember . . . that 'likely' and 'probable' are
> value-words; in many contexts 'It is probable (or likely) that
> P.' is adequately rendered by 'There is *good* reason (or evidence)
> for holding that P' (p. 60),

shows very clearly whither we are wending; and after a series
of examples to support the conclusion that 'all decisions except
those, if any, that are completely arbitrary, are decisions of
principle' (p. 65) we are confronted with the pronouncement
that 'to make a value-judgement is to make a decision of
principle' (p. 70).

As far back as page 3 the value judgement was placed in the
class 'Prescriptive Language'; but to what dire destination that
deceptive label was in fact directing it we only now begin to
discover: A value judgement is a *decision*. I call the label
deceptive because a decision, being a psychological event, is
no part of *language*, and if to make a value judgement is to make
a decision then a value judgement as such does not belong
to language; it is not a communication of any kind; it is not
an utterance at all—not even a prescriptive utterance, let alone
a statement!

However, to quote from a famous illustrated nursery classic,

'*This looks like the end; but it isn't.*' The value judgement survives the mortal-seeming blow and is allowed to resume its place in language. Nevertheless its status as a communication has been sadly diminished; for Hare's assertion, afterwards modified but never retracted, that to make a value judgment is to make a decision of principle only allows it, on the most favourable view, to express a purely subjective attitude. And at this stage we begin to see where the alleged prescriptive element in value judgements fits into the general pattern.

This is best explained, I think, in a sentence I am about to quote which in substance affirms the private decision-making aspect of the value judgement whilst repeating the claim that it belongs among imperatives and not indicatives. The sentence follows shortly after a statement that 'it is the purpose of the word "good" and other value words to be used for teaching standards . . .' (p. 134) and it runs,

> To teach a person—or to decide on for oneself—a standard for judging the merits of objects of a certain class is to teach or decide on principles for choosing between objects of that class (p. 134).

Accordingly the argument, as I understand it, amounts to this: To say to oneself 'That is a good so-and-so' is to make—or presumably to reaffirm—a personal decision of principle; if on the other hand these words are said to somebody else the word 'good' is being used to teach a standard, which is to teach a principle for choosing. But in order to use it thus the speaker must have made his decision of principle first, so that what is taught by his use of the word 'good' depends on the teacher's decision of principle as previously made and not on any possible objective significance of the word 'good'. In this way the arbitrary, imperative aspect of the spoken value judgement is finally established: a spoken value judgement is a kind of command (though this harsh-seeming conclusion has been softened in advance, we recall, by the argument that the 'function' of a command is not really to produce the action commanded). So now any claim on behalf of the spoken value judgement that it can be *objectively informative* is finally disposed of, and it is relegated to the position of a prescriptive utterance based on a private evaluation decision. (It is still, however, allowed *some* 'descriptive' meaning, as we shall see; but I will deal with this aspect later on.)

Now it is very noticeable that once the subjective and non-verbal character of the value-judgement—as a decision—has entered the discussion, the inquiry turns increasingly towards matters of motive, choice, and the various personal reasons there may be for making these judgements in various circumstances, so that what began as an exercise in language-analysis merges with an inquiry into states of mind. This kind of thing seems to happen unfailingly with every exposition of an ethical theory that tries to connect open value language with moral-value judgements, and I do not think it is difficult to see why. But before saying any more about this it will be convenient to look at the way psychology enters into Mr. Hare's treatment of what he distinguishes as specifically *moral* value judgements or decisions, and the principles to which they relate.

9

In reference to stated principles such as 'Never say what is false', decision is again mentioned, and called 'a factor (in our reasoning about conduct) which is of the very essence of morals' (pp. 54–55). This occurs after the view that moral judgements can be inferred from statements about the world has been very thoroughly disposed of. (Earlier there is an endorsing reference to 'Hume's celebrated observation on the impossibility of deducing an "ought"-proposition from a series of "is"-propositions', followed at once, however, by the assertion that the 'basis' of Hume's observation is 'that if to say something is good is to guide action then it cannot be merely to state a fact about the world' (p. 29). (If this is meant to be an interpretation of Hume's underlying meaning it is distinctly arbitrary, seeing that his celebrated observation does not mention 'good' at all.) Mr Hare makes his point about decisions as follows:

> When somebody says either 'This is false, so I won't say it', or 'This is false but I'll say it all the same and make an exception to my principle', he is doing a lot more than inferring . . . Inferring consists in saying that if he tells a falsehood he will be breaking the principle, whereas if he tells the truth he will be observing it . . . The rest of what he does is not inference at

all but something quite different, namely, deciding whether to alter the principle or not.

And he concludes, 'What we have to investigate is, not some looseness of the entailment, but *the way in which we form and modify our principles*' [my italics] 'and the relation between this process and the particular decisions that we make in the course of it' (p. 55).

10

This conclusion seems to me perfectly correct. In order to understand moral principles we have to investigate psychological and perhaps also sociological questions. For the way in which a man forms and modifies his principles and makes his decisions depends on such factors as the group into which he was born, his individual upbringing, his personal experiences, his innate disposition—whether it is that of a rebel or a conformist—in short upon a multitude of personal factors that language has nothing to do with at all.

The fact is that *there is no open language of moral evaluation* (see Chapter 4, sections 13–14 above); and Hare himself brings out this point with two examples to show the essential subjectivity of moral-value judgements. One is that of a parson who says that a certain girl is 'a good girl'. We infer what sort of character this denotes because we know the speaker's occupation: 'We may expect her to go to church, for example' (p. 146). Another case is that of a Christian among head-hunters who are surprised because he commends as 'good' not the man who collects a large number of heads, but the man who is meek and gentle (p. 148). In both these cases, it is emphasized, the word 'good' is, as always, a word of *commendation*, but what it stands for depends on the speaker's personal idea (however acquired) of what constitutes moral goodness in a person. What does this mean? That unless we know what sort of individual, with what sort of moral 'background', is passing the judgement we cannot know what is being asserted. The words 'good' and 'bad' that he uses are mere words of commendation and discommendation, and even if it should be claimed that they must reflect some accepted principle or other, because *all* types of statement do that (see section 8 above), the conclusion remains inescapable

that all they do *as language* is to express an attitude of favour
or disfavour. Thus as with decisions of principle, so with moral
value judgements on people and their actions, it is ultimately
a matter of individual attitude; and in the case of spoken moral-
value judgements we have to know who is speaking, minimally
what sort of person is speaking, before we can guess the meaning
of what he says, over and above the emotional attitude expressed in it. Thus the words 'good' and 'bad' as applied to
people and actions are reduced to the level of smiles and
frowns, and what we have to know so as to understand them is
something about the psychology of the speaker.

> The sentences in which (the moral words) appear are normally
> the expression of decisions of principle (p. 77). . . . ought-sen-
> tences . . . can only be verified by reference to a standard
> or a set of principles which we have by our own decision
> accepted and made our own (pp. 77–78).

They can only be 'verified', that is, by referring to the individual
speaker's personal moral values, however acquired.

The two passages just quoted I have as a matter of fact
ruthlessly wrenched from their contexts, which would reveal
that they were by no means intended to make the points they
do actually make. The purpose here was to persuade us that
it is more admirable, more 'adult', to *select* our principles of
conduct from among those offered to us by other people, than
to take them over unquestioningly. This reflects a personal
value judgement on the author's part which most readers will
no doubt agree with; but it also underlines the point that every
spoken moral-value judgement can only reflect a personal
moral 'decision'.

Except that he tried to make every personal moral decision
a decision in conformity with a law the individual regards as
universally willable, Kant reached the same conclusion, and
Hare invokes his support for it:

> As Kant saw, judgements which are properly moral must rest
> upon the property the will has of being a law to itself (inde-
> pendently of every property belonging to the objects of
> volition) (p. 196).

Kant, however, insisted that the individual's sense of Duty
was the ultimate determinant, thus closing a breach which Hare

leaves open by allowing the consideration of consequences to enter into the moral decision: e.g. 'The whole point about a decision is that it makes a difference to what happens: and this difference is the difference between the effects of deciding one way and the effects of deciding the other' (p. 57).

This means that the consideration of what will happen as the result of the decision being made effective is material to any moral decision. Kant would not have this, because he saw that to admit the consideration of consequences into the moral decision would be to break down the distinction between prudential and disinterested decisions, or between categorical and hypothetical 'imperatives'.

II

Duty in the Kantian sense Mr Hare brushes aside in a curious passage which seems to be an attempt to dissolve the difference between Duty in the key moral sense of the word, and 'duty' meaning simply job or function. In reference to the judgement 'You ought to tell the truth' he says that in this case we can substitute for 'You ought' 'It is your duty', whereas in 'You ought to give a second dose' said to a would-be poisoner we cannot. This, he says, 'is because the word "duty" is restricted in respect of the classes of comparison within which it is used to commend; it is used almost exclusively for moral duties, legal duties, military duties, and other duties belonging to a particular station' (p. 162).

Thus, bewilderingly, 'moral duties' are classed along with 'duties belonging to a particular station', apparently in order to avoid recognizing the exclusive *moral* meaning of Duty, central in Kant, which rigorously separates the moral from the non-moral evaluation of actions. Kant, because he insisted that moral decisions must be made regardless of aims or ends, could in theory have left psychology out of his analysis after he had laid down his two formal conditions that to be moral an act must not be inspired by an aim, and that it must be done 'from Duty', and in fact his excursions into psychology only tended to weaken his position (see Chapter 5, section 7 above). But for one who, like Hare, rejects the Kantian criterion, whilst at the same time claiming that moral-value judgements on people

M

and actions have something distinctive about them which makes them different from, e.g., efficiency-evaluations, there is nothing left to mark the distinction except the feelings of the person who passes the judgement—which leads to the sort of speculations about the motives underlying moral judgements (or spoken moral decisions) in which this work abounds.

For the *language* of moral evaluation, with its 'good', 'bad', 'right', 'wrong', and 'ought' happens to be identical with the language of non-moral evaluation, and if there is to be no moral touchstone-term such as Kant's 'Duty' against which value statements can be tested, *there is nothing in language to tell us which is which*. Hare attempts to get over this trouble by distinguishing the moral-value judgement as a special kind of prescriptive utterance among other prescriptive utterances— the kind, namely, which is about people and actions. But this is not enough, because he recognizes that not all value judgements passed on people and actions *are* moral in any sense which differentiates them from value judgements passed on other things: '"He is a good man" may not be a moral judgement; for "man" may be an abbreviation for ... "man to put in to bat first"' (p. 162). That is, they may be efficiency-evaluations. This might indeed have been got over by decreeing that to say 'A is a good man', meaning that he is a good cricketer, is a misuse of language, and similarly that to say 'That was a good action' when the meaning is that it was a good stroke of business is likewise impermissible. I think such a rule would have some justification in accepted ideas of correct usage, and that it would have improved the situation in some respects. But it would not have met the main difficulty, which is not over the object on which the judgement is passed, but over what the judgement itself means. If 'good man' means, as Hare says, 'man to try to become like' (p. 144) in a properly moral judgement, then what sort of man that is, depends upon the speaker's moral 'tastes' in men: and the same applies to actions. The moral-value judgement remains intractably private and personal.

I think it is now easy to understand why in a study of this kind, which seeks to interpret the language of moral judgement, which is one thing, by analysing open value-language, which is another thing, the lines of inquiry are bound to cross, psychology will become entangled with the discussion of meanings, and the result will be unsatisfactory both logically and psychologically; showing once again that language analysis and psychological analysis cannot be carried on satisfactorily in the same laboratory.

12

In the present case the conclusion must be, on Mr Hare's own premises, that there can be no objective test for the goodness of men or actions. And this he concedes—in effect—as follows:

> ... when we are speaking of a good act we are speaking of the act as indicative of the goodness of the man; and the choices that we are seeking to guide are ... those of people who are asking themselves 'What sort of man ought I to try to become?' (p. 186).

This cannot be denied—for who are 'we'? But in so far as it is so, to speak of the goodness of a man or an act is to speak a special language, a kind of moral-code-language, altogether different from open value language.

This conclusion is of course not the one Mr Hare intended to reach, for his contention that 'moral judgements provide reasons for acting in one way and not in another' (p. 197) rests, not upon any definition of specifically *moral* reasons, but upon arguments all directed to showing that moral judgements, being value-judgements, are all of a piece with other, non-moral, value-judgements, the only difference being that they relate to matters—people and conduct—on which we feel deeply:

> We get stirred up about the goodness of men because we are men. This means that the acceptance of the judgement that such-and-such a man's act is good in circumstances of a certain sort, involves the acceptance of the judgement that it would be good, were we ourselves placed in similar circumstances, to do likewise (p. 141).

This is part of an argument directed *against* the view that 'the use of the word "good" in moral contexts is totally different from its use in non-moral ones' (p. 140), leading to the conclusion that the ultimate difference is only in the degree and kind of emotion felt in the one case and in the other. Which again emphasizes that where Duty is left out of the reckoning the difference between moral and non-moral judgements is a difference in the feelings of those who make them, and not any difference of language; in fact that there is no distinctive 'language of morals' at all.

13

That Mr Hare, like other moral philosophers, has failed in his attempt to give us a satisfactory account of moral evaluation is a matter for Ethicists to lament if they will. But that his method in making this attempt was first to lay violent hands upon everyday non-moral value language is the concern of the axiologist, and here lies my quarrel with his book. I accuse Mr Hare of attempting to drag down to the level of mere moral judgements a language—the language of non-moral evaluation—which is of the highest importance in open communication: an importance which would be far more widely recognized than it is if it were not for the well-meant activities of the moral philosophers. Before I go on with my indictment let me briefly recall what Mr Hare does initially to the non-moral value statement, and how he sets about breaking it in so that it can be made to draw the chariot of Morals.

To begin with, the value statement is deprived of its objectivity, by being classified as an expression of commendation or discommendation, and is further subdued by being branded as a decision. This makes even its claim to be an utterance doubtful, so that sometimes it has to be merely a private psychological event tied to a principle. At all times it is compelled to serve as an answer to a question, equally whether it is being used to predicate goodness or badness of such diverse things as fruit, cars, and human actions. Thus any informative power the value statement may be allowed to enjoy is completely subordinated to its function of recommending types of action in accordance with the principles held at the time by the person who pronounces it. These, then, are the main features of Mr Hare's general treatment of the value statement containing the word 'good', which is the type he concentrates on.

Mr Hare tries to support his claim that a conduct-guiding imperative or choice-guiding exhortation is wrapped up in every goodness-statement by exhibiting various instances of ordinary value statements which, he finds, all contain this element; but really this is as superfluous as it is unconvincing, seeing that it has been decreed beforehand that all 'value judgements' do have this characteristic, and that it has been made a matter of definition by placing the value statement under the heading of *prescriptive* language; in addition to which there are frequent reminders such as the following,

> I have said that the primary function of the word 'good' is to commend . . . When we commend or condemn anything, it is always in order, at least indirectly, to guide choices, our own or other people's, now or in the future (p. 127).

Nevertheless, as well as its essentially prescriptive or imperative function the value statement is allowed by Mr Hare to have some degree of *descriptive* meaning, though in this concession the claim for the primacy of the *prescriptive* element moults no feather. The concession that value statements may have descriptive meaning is based on recognition of the 'undoubted fact of usage' (p. 118), that they are often used for descriptive purposes—though what sort of description they convey when so used depends, as we have been told, not only on the context of the statement and the kind of object it is about, but also on the speaker's decisions of principle, as well as on how far his hearer knows or shares them (see section 10 above).

Now, all the goodness-statements Mr Hare instances in a chapter headed 'Description and Evaluation' belong to the class of those in which, on my interpretation, 'good' stands for 'functionally satisfactory' (see Chapter 2, section 9); and in this chapter it is only in one place, with one example, that he in effect recognizes that this might be the actual, and the sole, meaning-content of a statement in the form 'That is a good so-and-so'—though logically considered his example is infelicitous: He conceeds here that the value statement 'That is a good motor-car' may be demonstrably *untrue*, which would mean, of course, that it is in its context an *objectively testable* statement; and the concession is justified as follows:

> It will be noticed that 'motor-car', unlike 'strawberry', is a functional word . . . Reference to the *Shorter Oxford English Dictionary* shows that a motor-car is a carriage, and a carriage a means of conveyance. Thus, if a motor-car will not convey anything, we know from the definition of motor-car that it is not a good one (p. 112).

One would have thought that the necessary conclusion, on *this* reasoning, would have been that 'That is a good motor-car' was untrue in this case because the object referred to was *not a motor-car at all*, and not because it was not a *good* motor-car. However, the inference clearly made here is that if a thing will not perform the function it is intended to perform it is not good; and its being not good inheres in its not being functionally satisfactory. (And by the same token, surely, if a strawberry is grown in order to be eaten and enjoyed, and it proves impossible to eat and enjoy it, then it is, in the same sense, not a good strawberry, just as with other things that are produced for our use; and whether or not their names are 'functional' has, clearly, nothing whatever to do with the case.) This is normal basic evaluation; it is part of open value language, and its foundation is the assumption that Anyone likes the things he wants to use to be satisfactorily usable. For Mr Hare to have recognized this here,[1] albeit grudgingly, and only in relation to motor-cars that won't go, was surprising. For it is quite apparent that this type of value 'judgement' is a *statement*, not a prescriptive utterance; not an oblique recommendation, but a testable proposition.

However, this aspect of the value statement, having been allowed to make a brief appearance, is pushed out of the way again, and the argument advances on its pre-destined course, the concession that a value judgement has 'descriptive meaning' being followed by passages of analysis to show that that meaning is subordinate to the prescriptive one, or that 'the descriptive meaning of "good" [is] secondary to the evaluative meaning' (p. 118). (For 'evaluative' read 'prescriptive'.) The contention is that even though we were to say that an object is good, and justify this by listing in detail all the characteristics to virtue of which we call it good this list would not be a full translation of the goodness-statement; some element would be missing, namely the essential prescriptive, or choice-guiding, element.

14

That a list of approved properties is not the whole meaning-

[1] In a different chapter there is mention of the judgement 'This is (is not) a good auger' (pp. 100–1) the purpose of which is to show the inadequacy as description of this type of statement.

content of a goodness-statement about an object of use is beyond dispute, because *it is not any of its meaning-content*; and I think that in the sense in which Mr Hare uses the term 'descriptive', no open value statement has any descriptiveness at all. All it does is to make a distinctive kind of testable assertion about the object, which according to context is the assertion that it is—or is not—functionally satisfactory, or that it is beneficent—or contra-beneficent or harmful—in some more general way. The statement 'That is a good chair' means only that it is a functionally satisfactory chair, and no part of the meaning of the statement is that it has these-or-those physical properties. 'Good' does not stand for 'made of strong materials' or for 'multiple-sprung'. Any list of the properties on account of which we say that it is a good chair lies outside the value-statement itself; just as any list of the properties on account of which we say that it is a strong or a fragile chair lies outside *that* statement, which can only be contradicted by saying that it is *not* a strong, or *not* a fragile chair. How we afterwards justify such statements, or how we came to make them in the first place, or why we ever made them at all, is quite another matter. Mr Hare rightly points out that '"Good" is a "super-venient" or "consequential" epithet' (p. 131). We call a thing good *because of* properties we think it possesses or tendencies we think it has, and our goodness-statements may be reversed or contradicted not *by* but *because of*, contrary evidence about those properties or tendencies. This is precisely because open evaluations, being dependent on the basic-values assumption, refer directly to the object as it may affect the relevant needs of people. (See Chapter 2, sections 4–7.) To ask for a list of the physical properties on account of which one has stated that something is good is to make a perfectly natural request for information, but it is *not* to ask for any part of the meaning of the word 'good' as used in the statement. Mr Hare, however, insists that it is, and pronounces that after the speaker has given an exhaustive list of the properties of the object in question, by way of break-ing down the meaning of the word 'good' in his statement, what he still has to include to produce a complete translation is his *commendation*, which feature, we are told quite arbitrarily, amounts to a command or an exhortation to choose the object or one like it, at least if the hearer is ever in a situation where

he intends to make an act of choice in respect to it or its like
(see the quotation in section 13 above). Continual emphasis is
laid on the fact that 'good' is used for commendation; but this,
after all, only gives it a characteristic in common with other
words of commendation like 'fab' and 'lovely', which may or
may not be incidentally informative (and to which no objective
data can have much relevance).

15

With the main theme of *The Language of Morals* I entirely agree
—indeed it is one of the main themes of my own book: value
language is of the utmost importance for guiding choices. But
I maintain that this is not because it can convey veiled commands, or because it enables us to express emotional attitudes
—for which purpose we have other means of expression, some
of which are not verbal at all—not yet because it reflects the
differing tastes and conventions prevailing within various
social groups. On the contrary, my claim for the importance
of value language—that is, *basic*-value language—rests on recognition of its unique service in enabling us to make a special
kind of *objective* statements, such that no matter who we are,
or where we live, and no matter whether we are considering
cars or actions or world-shaking events, our language can reflect
ideas of *beneficence* and *harmfulness* which are so widely shared
that, as with ideas about physical matters of fact, they can be
translated from one tongue into another, and canvassed in
terms which 'anyone' understands. In this way value language
gives us, all of us, the means to discuss and to reach decisions
on what to do for our individual and our common advantage.

The language of open, basic evaluation allows propositions of
beneficence, c-b, and harmfulness to be debated and tested,
whether they concern small objects or great, small matters or
great, *so long as the value terms used are kept free of contamination by
ethical ideas.* But where these corruptions of meaning creep in,
and 'good' may mean 'Good', expressing a moral attitude—the
outcome of who-knows-what personal quirks and complexes—
the language of evaluation loses its usefulness as a department of
communication, and good will is bereft of one of its most
valuable instruments.

9
SOME EFFECTS OF THE
MORAL ATTITUDE

> *Many of the worst crimes in history have been committed*
> *by men who had a strong sense of duty, just because*
> *their sense of duty was so strong.*
> P. H. NOWELL-SMITH

SUMMARY: Because of the refusal of most moral philosophers to accept Kant's strict demarcation between
ethical and non-ethical evaluation, moral philosophy is
now permeated with the stultifying influence of Moralism. Most prescriptive teaching is moralistic, in that
it associates the notion of good action with that of Duty
and absolute Rightness. I give reasons for regarding
the effect of this teaching as harmful: It fosters the belief
that doing good is closely connected with—or even
necessarily involves—self-sacrifice; which belief tends
to discourage good action. It denies by implication
that one may act from a *desire* to benefit others. It impedes
the recognition of *common interests*. I take Polanyi's
criticism of Locke's doctrine of liberty to illustrate the
authoritarian consequences of the view—upheld by both
—that all good or socially desirable behaviour occurs
in obedience to divine (transcendental) moral laws; and
also to show that the concept of a transcendent Rightness
and the Duty to uphold it may override principles of
conduct which experience has shown to be good, i.e.
beneficent. I give it as my personal opinion that in terms
of basic evaluation the ethico-moralistic approach to
problems of conduct does more *harm* than *good*, but
concede that various arguments, *likewise in 'basic' terms*,
might be advanced to the opposite effect. My chief aim
has been to show that basic evaluation allows us to debate
this question objectively by the light of human experience.

N

I

In the course of these chapters I think it has emerged that the subject called Ethics or Moral Philosophy is permeated with Moralism, and that Moralism is a muddle and a begetter of muddles. Yet Moral Philosophy is still greatly respected. People think of it as the store-house of wisdom about questions of ultimate importance to us all, and seem hardly to have noticed that it has been steadily degenerating into the most sterile of philosophical subjects, occupied with niggling word-games or portentous debates on matters which even the sacred word 'principle' can't redeem from triviality.

Only think, for example, of the celebrated 'concert-ticket problem', first raised about fifteen years ago and revived on countless occasions since. This problem, it may be remembered, was stated as follows: 'Supposing I had one ticket for a concert, and supposing X would appreciate the concert just as much as I, but no more: ought I to give him my ticket or go myself?' That the debate could go on *ad infinitum* was, of course, due to the simple fact, long ago noted by Kant, that 'ought' has both an ethical and a non-ethical (advisory) sense. The only possible answer to the problem in properly ethical terms is that it depends what the individual ticket-holder's sense of Duty dictates, and that what it dictates he Ought to do. If, for instance, he is imbued with a sense of the Duty of self-sacrifice he Ought obviously to give away the ticket. In non-ethical terms there can be no general theoretical problem, seeing that we don't know the circumstances under which 'I' have to decide, nor what 'my' relevant motives are supposed to be: How much do I want to 'spread joy around'; do I or do I not want to feel, or to appear, unselfish? Do I expect a long-term advantage through giving away the ticket? It would be necessary to know all this and probably much more before venturing to give an individual advisory opinion.

The ambiguity of 'ought' is an inexhaustible source of problems in Ethics such as dons delight to sieze and worry: 'Ought' we to keep our promises in all circumstances? How if the promise were to injure somebody? Can it ever *be* a moral obligation to inflict injury, and if so when? 'Right' and 'wrong', too, are just as fertile in futilities. Have we a 'right' to punish—

to take life—or, more specifically, to use the H-bomb? And so on, and so on.

Yet moral philosophy, I repeat, is still held in respect, and it may not lose that respect even though it too often seems to be almost entirely preoccupied with crossword puzzles that in the nature of things can never be solved. But the result may not be happy. For intellectual frivolity in high places, even though not recognized as what it is, has a stultifying effect on the minds of ordinary people in the long run, which makes them less capable of thinking intelligently, and so constructively, about practical problems, so that they are the more likely to come to harm. These perhaps rather platitudinous remarks sum up my main indictment of academic Moralism, but they are not quite all I have to say by way of evaluative footnote to what has gone before.

Before I continue, a point about terminology: Moralism is the offspring of ambiguous relations between pure Ethics and vulgar values, but it bears the name and wears the mantle of Ethics, and Ethics is by most serious-minded people regarded as a good thing. So in deference to established usage I shall, as before, use 'Ethics' and 'ethical' in the looser sense—where 'morality' and 'moral' seem less appropriate—in discussing this view.

2

Let it be said once more that exhortations to do good may lead to good being done. Nobody would wish to deny this, or to deny that people with a strong sense of Duty often lead valuable and exemplary lives.

Such facts are so much taken for granted, however, that there is little point in dwelling on them here, and as in this final phase of the present discussion my chief object is to act as Devil's Advocate against the great body of those dedicated to the view that ethical values are the indispensable basis of all human goodness and good behaviour, I will only mention one further respect in which the moral attitude seems undoubtedly to be in a 'particular limited' way beneficent. I refer to that special kind of spiritual security that moral conviction can give. People who 'know the difference between Right and Wrong' have a stability and confidence which is not the same thing as self-righteousness—since those who have these certainties will admit that they often do Wrong—but which is a strong support in the face of life's terrible and daunting complexities. Such people feel that they have something far more reliable than their own fallible intelligence to guide them in making decisions; and this is a very real blessing, especially in times of such anxiety and uncertainty as our own:

> To humbler functions, awful Power!
> I call thee: I myself commend
> Unto thy guidance from this hour;
> O, let my weakness have an end!
>
> Give unto me, made lowly wise
> The spirit of self-sacrifice;
> The confidence of reason give;
> And in the light of truth thy
>   bondman let me live!

The reference to 'reason' in Wordsworth's 'Ode to Duty' is perhaps an echo from Kant; but the whole spirit is that of one who turns away from reasoning to intuition and the comfort of the inner voice which will infallibly give the Right answer. So much at least, then, to the credit of Duty. Like religion it can afford deep spiritual comfort to the anxious and perplexed. Now for the indictment.

3

In terms of basic values the most direct challenge to the claim of unqualified goodness for anything is to ask: Does it cause or promote avoidable suffering? The answer with regard to the ethical or moral attitude is, of course, that it does very often. Among the most implacable Duties are those deriving from religious faith, and high among these may stand the Duty of making life unbearable for the unbeliever and the heretic.

In the past the mutual persecutions carried on by Christian sects proceeded in an atmosphere of unrelenting moral righteousness on the part of everybody, and the torment and slaughter of thousands was justified by the absolute obligation to enforce observance of this or that detail of ritual, or acceptance of this or that interpretation of an ambiguous passage of scripture. But in the course of time the emphasis shifted, crude bigotry receded, and religious teaching began to dwell less upon outward observances and more upon moral principles of a general kind. Yet in spite of the increasing concentration on the spirit rather than the letter of the scriptures, ecclesiastical bodies still claimed the God-given right to exercise their authority to whatever extent they considered necessary, even if in fact this was no longer always feasible, and—the point I want particularly to make here—they were, and still are, able to support this claim by invoking traditional assumptions about human nature which the moral attitude fosters and which, because of the prevalence of moral piety, have mostly passed unchallenged to this day. I refer especially to the acceptance of Saint Augustine's doctrine that all human goodness comes from a supernatural source. This view, though it is often repudiated even by Christian Ethicists, has been preserved in the idea, by no means confined to churchmen, that man's sense of his Duty to obey a divinely given law is, if not the only, at least by far the most effective, agency of decent, social, civilized behaviour.

4

Now setting aside the question of its plausibility—and of course there is no way of actually disproving it any more than of proving it—anyone must see that the above notion is bound to have very serious effects on our whole social outlook. It amounts to believing that it is unusual and difficult, if not impossible, to be good 'of our own accord'. In fact it amounts to the extremest pessimism about human nature—no notion could well be more discouraging. But further, the idea that we cannot be good without supernatural assistance can be observed to influence our thinking about the relations between man and man no less than between man and God, and in ways which can have widespread practical consequences. Some of these consequences are, I think, demonstrably harmful:

spiritual bullying, or even physical coercion; and that kind of mind-darkening which comes of belief in Powers ruling our lives and demanding unquestioning submission.

It is easy to pretend that all this sort of thing belongs to the past and that 'we' have learnt the arts of moderation and compromise well enough to protect us against the worst excesses of piety. But it may be as well to realize that so long as the beliefs which have always been the ultimate justification for religious persecution are still present and strong, the mischief, though dormant, may always break out afresh in favourable circumstances; and there are plenty of these at the present time.

5

The peculiarly insidious effect of assuming a supernatural source of human goodness, and how this assumption may be used for the ends of authoritarianism is very well shown, I think, in an attack on spiritual liberty published in our own day which tellingly exploits, of all things, the libertarian arguments of John Locke. I give this as the best example I can find to show how essentially vulnerable any libertarian doctrine must be if its author still clings to any version of the belief that the laws of good behaviour come to us from Above, or, to put it in terms of the present discussion, that human goodness and Goodness are one and the same.

Though Locke endorsed this view in various of his writings he was a tolerant man, and he held that it becomes Christians to refrain from ill-treating those who dissent from their opinions:

> The toleration of those, that differ from others, in matters of religion, is so agreeable to the gospel of Jesus Christ, and to the genuine reason of mankind, that it seems monstrous for men to be so blind as not to perceive the necessity and advantage of it, in so clear a light.[1]

It evidently did not occur to Locke that his arguments for the agreement of divine authority with his own civilized standards,

[1] A Letter Concerning Toleration. *The Works of John Locke* (1751) Vol. II, p. 244.

including respect for the other fellow's point of view, might by minds of a different bent from his own be taken to point in precisely the opposite direction. In his own day Locke's ecclesiastical critics attacked him for saying that religious and moral convictions are not innate but acquired, and for citing in support of this the great variety of moral ideas obtaining in various parts of the world at various periods—as if to say, forsooth, that one set of moral principles was as good as another! But for present purposes it is more interesting to see what became of his arguments in the formidable hands of Professor Michael Polanyi, the ingenious author of a work published in 1951 entitled *The Logic of Liberty*.

In his *Essay on the Human Understanding* Locke's plea for religious toleration as set forth in the famous Letters is conveniently summarized as follows:

> Since ... it is unavoidable to the greatest part of men, if not all, to have several opinions, without certain and indubitable proofs of their truths ... it would, methinks, become all men to maintain peace and the common offices of humanity and friendship in the diversity of opinions ... We should do well to commiserate our mutual ignorance, and endeavour to remove it in all the gentle and fair ways of information, and not instantly treat others ill as obstinate and perverse because they will not renounce their own and receive our opinions, or at least those we would force upon them, when it is more than probable that we are no less obstinate in not embracing some of theirs.[1]

Locke maintained that religious ideas are matters of faith 'without certain and indubitable proofs of their truth', and that such ideas cannot be altered by force, though they may be modified by the light of reason. Professor Polanyi fastens upon this argument for the tolerant treatment of those whose religious opinions differ from our own, in order to illustrate what he calls 'an internal contradiction in the doctrine of liberty':

> The argument of doubt put forward by Locke in favour of tolerance says that since it is impossible to demonstrate which religion is true, we should admit them all. This implies that we must not impose beliefs that are not demonstrable. Let us apply this doctrine to ethical principles. It follows that unless ethical

[1] Op. cit. Book IV, Chapter XVI, p. 4.

principles can be demonstrated with certainty we should refrain
from imposing them and should tolerate their denial. But, of
course, ethical principles cannot be demonstrated: you cannot
prove the obligation to tell the truth, to uphold justice and
mercy. It would follow therefore that a system of mendacity,
lawlessness and cruelty is to be accepted as an alternative
to ethical principles on equal terms. But a society in which
unscrupulous propaganda, violence and terror prevail offers
no scope for tolerance. Here the inconsistency of a liberalism
based on philosophic doubt becomes apparent: freedom of
thought is destroyed by the extension of doubt to traditional
ideals.[1]

6

Here then is a justification of religious intolerance which makes
cunning use of Locke's own reasons for opposing it.

Now the thing to notice is that the unstated assumption on
which Professor Polanyi bases his argument from analogy is
that ethical principles which, like religious beliefs, are absolute
and undemonstrable, are all that prevents us from embracing,
if ever we feel so disposed, 'a system of mendacity, lawlessness,
and cruelty'; and just in so far as Locke agrees with Professor
Polanyi's view that a divine Law is the ultimate source of those
absolute ethical principles which, allegedly, alone prevent us
from adopting 'a system' requiring us to act like juvenile
delinquents or Nietzschean supermen, it does follow that if good
principles are to be preserved some authority must be empowered to 'impose'—sinister term—the supernatural beliefs
that alone enable the deliverances of the divine legislator to
be heard. If it is true, as Locke himself maintains in another
place, that 'the duties of [God's] law, arising from the constitution of His nature, are of eternal obligation' and that this
law cannot be 'taken away, or dispensed with, without changing
the nature of things, overturning the measures of right and
wrong, and thereby introducing and authorizing irregularity,
confusion, and disorder in the world'[2] the fact that this Rule
is not demonstrable does not alter the situation any more than
does the undemonstrability of transcendent truths. Locke com-

---

[1] *The Logic of Liberty*, p. 97.
[2] The Reasonableness of Christianity, op. cit. Vol. II, p. 563.

mitted himself in such passages to the orthodox Christian view, shared by all sects, that the source of good action is not human will and judgement, but man's sense of Duty to obey a divine authority; and he thus gave a valuable opening to an astute opponent of religious toleration.

The point I want to emphasize is that it is *only* the assumption that undemonstrable and primary ethical rules are the ultimate source of good conduct-principles which produces the 'internal contradiction in the doctrine of liberty' which Professor Polanyi has discovered. And it should be noticed that no such contradiction is necessarily involved in Locke's theism by itself. For he could simply have maintained that God, the author of our being, has endowed us with reason in order that we shall decide for ourselves with the help of experience what to do so as to find happiness in this world and win salvation in the next. He does in a score of places argue to just this effect, but nearly always, with exasperating inconsistency, he also declares that holy writ or divine revelation are the ultimate authorities: 'the unchanging rule of right and wrong which the law of God hath established.' Since divine revelations and passages of scripture may convey various, or even downright contradictory, truths to different people, truths which are undemonstrable and irrefutable by either test or argument, Locke does seem in effect to be unintentionally endorsing the usual excuse of Christian sects, with their differing interpretations of God's laws, for persecuting each other whenever they are strong enough. (To be sure, this is not precisely how Professor Polanyi expresses what he is advocating, but his conclusions from Locke's premises amount, on analysis, to nothing less.)

There is no disputing the skill of this attack on tolerance, in its neat exploitation of ethico-moralistic assumptions. For in our own time, no less than in Locke's, numbers of serious-minded and well-intentioned people go even further than did Locke himself, in ascribing *all* social virtues, and *all* humane standards to a Higher agency than human will and judgement. Such people approve of the standards, they recognize them as good and want to preserve them, but having been taught that the goodness of these standards originates neither in good will nor in reason, but in a transcendent and absolute Goodness, their minds are ripe to succumb to the doctrine that in order

to preserve the standards, priests and other divinely-appointed
leaders—those few men who are, as it were, in the confidence
of the Absolute—must be empowered to *impose* their dogmas
on the rest of us, in order that by being Good we shall also be
good.

7

This very same disposition to bow before the Absolute can of
course be exploited by the apostles of other dogmas besides
those of the Christian churches. With gruesome priggishness
the Communist 'intellectual' invokes 'the ethics of inevitability'
to justify extremes of spiritual and physical tyranny in the name
of a sacred Historical Process. 'We must accept the direction of
evolution as good simply because it *is* good according to any
realist definition of that concept' C. H. Waddington once
wrote. Professor Waddington was writing not as a Marxist,
which he is not, but as an exponent of Evolutionist Ethics. But
his words could equally well serve as a motto for the high priests
of dialectical materialism. For all the up-to-date flavour of the
saying, a very long tradition has sanctified just this kind of
moralistically ambiguous use of the term 'good', and one does
not need much imagination to see how useful the resulting
befuddlement of the public mind can be to established or
aspiring dictators. There is hardly a form of tyranny or cruelty
that some ethical school or other cannot be found to bless, on
the ground that it serves the ends of some great Process or
Will which is bound in the end to prevail. And so also, under
the banner of Duty—to a God or a Process or a personified
Nation—power-avid leaders pursue their narrow ends and are
applauded as saints and saviours.

8

The passage I have quoted from Professor Michael Polanyi's
authoritarian tract can serve to illustrate another point which
is relevant to the present inquiry.

It might have been expected that Professor Polanyi would
be perfectly capable of recognizing how sophistical was the use

¹ *Science and Ethics*, p. 18.

he made of Locke's argument. But in fact it is quite evident that his zeal blinded him, and that at the time of writing he genuinely believed that for the sake of enjoying liberty—to an unspecified degree—we must submit to coercion—to an unspecified degree—by religious authorities, because the beliefs they would 'impose' on us embody certain absolute moral standards, without which we should be no better than the beasts.

But now let us ask, supposing some devout believer, writing to the same effect, *had* noticed the tendenciousness of his own argument, and that he really recognized the existence of stronger inducements to civilized conduct than the claims of religious absolutism. Could he, as a Christian moralist convinced of his Duty to uphold the faith, have allowed *any* considerations to deter him from advancing that argument and pressing those claims if only he believed that all this would be convincing and effective? The history of religious propaganda hardly encourages one to think so; and this is only natural. For to the extent that a man is convinced that his ultimate Duty is to a God or to a religious body, or indeed to *anything at all*, the claims of that Duty must be felt by him to override all other claims, whether those of personal advantage, or of benevolence or, equally, of those standards of intellectual integrity and fairness in debate which men of learning normally value highly and do their best to preserve. It can hardly be too often emphasized that Duty may demand *any* sort of conduct, and that whilst by its very nature it must neglect all the aims and inclinations of the moral agent himself it must, except when it happens to dictate beneficence, be equally indifferent to those of anybody else. Consequently it may be an absolute Duty of the moral man to destroy or betray things which others, and even he himself, hold to be good.

9

To end this inquiry I will very briefly suggest a few considerations about the possible psychological effects of ethical teaching.

It is so widely taken for granted that unless a child grows up with a strong sense of Duty he is certain to be an unreliable, unprincipled, and generally worthless member of society that any suggestion to the contrary is apt to be received as nothing

but an irritating attempt to be 'clever'. Yet anyone who thinks
for himself must surely at least recognize that the possession
of a sense of Duty is not a guarantee of good behaviour, and
that there may be other causes of good behaviour than the
possession of a sense of Duty. As Kant himself acknowledged,
it is quite usual for people to be honest and truthful on practical
grounds, and because for one reason and another they prefer
to be so. If a child learns the practical advantages and the
social importance of truthfulness he will normally speak the
truth, but he will not make veracity into a cast-iron fetish. (As
Schopenhauer remarked, and as many people would agree,
'Kant would have done better to open the vials of his wrath on
that vice which takes pleasure in seeing others suffer; it is
the latter, and not falsehood, which is truly fiendish'.) A disadvantage of making truthfulness a Duty is that if anything
should happen which makes lying the obviously necessary
course, the person who lies even from the most humane motives
will have to suffer the pains of 'moral' guilt.

10

The idea that Duty can be painful is nothing new. The idea
that it is sublime has been well stressed by Kant and others.
The idea that it makes people good has hardly ever been dis-
puted, still less *tested*. And here one fact positively clamours to
be pointed out: a fact which in one sort of context is vehemently
affirmed, but one which seems to be completely forgotten the
moment anyone questions the claim of Duty to be an effective
agency of goodness:

Despite the moral teaching, the notions of Right, Wrong,
Ought, and Duty which it is usual to impress upon children
from their earliest years, a considerable number of them have
always grown up to be very bad people. Now it is apt to be
taken for granted that such people are as they are because
for one reason or another their minds were not sufficiently
imbued with absolute moral ideals in childhood. Yet what
real justification is there for assuming this until the experiment
has been tried of bringing up children with the kind of non-
moralistic inducements to goodness which are normally in use,
whilst carefully shielding them from the influence of Duty-

imperatives; and then later comparing their characters and behaviour with those of a similar set of the Duty-trained? No doubt this is an unpractical suggestion, but until tests of this kind have been made, with results tending to confirm the Moralist's pre-suppositions, it is futile to complain at one and the same time about all the human wickedness which exists *in spite of* the clear lessons of Duty, and about the lack of Duty-consciousness in the young as the cause of the wickedness.

11

Setting aside the question of wickedness, however, we have plenty of evidence to support the view that normal natures respond to various practical inducements to behave well, at least as much as to moral exhortations.

Throughout our childhood we all find it very often necessary, both through the pressure of brute circumstances and of our elders, to control many of our impulses, and we come to understand that it is not always the best plan to do just whatever we happen to feel like doing at the time. Positive desires too play their part. For if we want to have friends we try to make people like us, and if we want to be trusted and respected we try to act so as to win confidence and respect. These are the kinds of inducement, along with the laws and conventions whose practical convenience we either learn from experience or take for granted, which help to make us acceptable members of society. Unfortunately they also compose the bandwaggon on which Ethics so impressively rides. And this brings us to what I believe to be a very dubious aspect of ethico-moralistic thinking.

12

It is a peculiarity of our culture that every voluntary act we perform, from the cradle to the grave, which is not inspired by hate, cruelty, or greed, is in danger of being placed to the credit of the moral Ought. Children are taught, and grow up still believing, that to be good is to be Moral, which is, in turn, to be self-denying; and that decent behaviour towards others is only possible through forgetfulness of self. Self-sacrifice is represented as a Duty, in direct opposition to the normal egoism

of the child, and he is told to think *not* of himself, *but* of others;
and so deeply has this poisonous antithesis entered some
people's minds that in face of all the facts of social give-and-
take they still entertain a vague belief that it is only through
harming oneself that one is ever able to do good. The effect
this has on the minds of those who are not particularly good-
natured, or imaginative about the suffering of their fellows,
may easily be guessed. How can they be got to believe that it
may be positively expedient to 'help foreigners', because this
will promote good feeling and diminish the chances of war,
if they have been brought up with the idea that to do good
to others is necessarily to do what is inexpedient? 'Charity
begins at home', is their knowing retort to any argument for
generous and far-sighted policies.

Another sort of mind is aware that it is often expedient rather
than moral to do good, but thanks to the influence of ethical
evaluation is inclined to discount the rewards of beneficence.
For to those who are responsive to the Kantian Duty-doctrine
the feeling that one has done Right is vastly more important
than the belief that one has done good, and the suggestion that
it may be *expedient*—in the Moralist's vocabulary a dirty word
—rather than moral, to cultivate helpful and harmonious
relations with our neighbours is shocking to minds in which
the ideas of self-sacrifice and goodness have once for all been
fused in their moral training. Brought up to identify virtue
with altruism, such people react with something near disgust
to the argument that it is not so much moral as worldly-wise
to be generous and just. For if this should be true, what is left
of one's scope for being nobly disinterested? Even if the service
of others should mean on occasions great trouble and inconvenience, and the renouncing of all sorts of immediate advantages, where is the moral merit in it, where the 'worthiness to
be happy', if all the time one really expects that it will be
worth while in the long run?

In this way the desire to be Good may operate as an actual
hindrance to good activity. Moreover, if this world is seen, as
by the Early Christians, chiefly as an arena for the performance
of self-sacrificing actions, one will not be very anxious to get
rid of the conditions which seem to call for them.

13

But finally, what is perhaps worst of all in the long run is the effect of the belief, nourished by constantly reiterated moral exhortations, that there is something 'unnatural' about good will and kindness; or at least that they are far less 'natural' than ill-will and unkindness.

In his ordering of motives the Moralist places self-regard and the desire for personal happiness into one compartment along with greed and aggressiveness, and into the compartment opposite he puts Duty and self-sacrifice with kindness and good will. That even Bentham, with his separate classification of 'self-regarding' and 'social' motives, came near to making this kind of mistake shows how deep-seated is the effect of this artificial antithesis between doing what is natural and doing what is beneficent. As Kant insisted, if Duty means anything it means the exclusion of all desires as determinants of our actions. The moral or dutiful act is by definition never the act that we wanted to do, and in stressing that it is our Duty to be kind the Moralist inevitably implies that we cannot *want* to relieve others' distress or promote their happiness. To this extent at least it seems safe to say that in terms of basic values the influence of ethical ideas is not good, seeing that their effect must be to impair faith in human good will, which, whether evoked by spontaneous distress at human suffering, or by the rational desire to make the world a better place for us all to live in, is probably the chief hope for humanity at the present time.

14

My conclusion is that on balance the ethical evaluation of motives and conduct, with its various effects on modes of thought and actions, does more harm than good. That is my personal opinion, based on considerations that I believe to be valid as far as they go. But I am quite sure there is a great deal to be said on the other side.

My chief purpose, however, has not been to convince anybody that ethical values in general do harm, but only to show that it is as feasible, as reasonable, and as useful to inquire into their value, as to inquire into the value of anything else that affects our lives.

INDEX